NEW FRONTIERS
OF KNOWLEDGE

ARNOLD TOYNBEE	JULES ROMAINS	CARLOS P. ROMULO
JOHN VON NEUMANN	MARGARET MEAD	DAVID SARNOFF
WILLIAM O. DOUGLAS	DE MADARIAGA	TOYOHIKO KAGAWA
PERCY BRIDGMAN	CARL GUSTAV JUNG	NATHAN M. PUSEY
HERMANN J. MULLER	ZAFRULLAH KAHN	WALT DISNEY
SIDNEY HOOK	BENJAMIN CARRION	HERBERT READ
CHARLES MALIK	COLIN CLARK	NELSON ROCKEFELLER
SUMNER SLICHTER	GUNNAR RANDERS	RAMASWAMI AIYAR
HENRY LUCE	FUAT KOPRULU	LEE DE FOREST
GILBERTO FREYRE	HOMI BHABHA	W. J. GIBBONS
WHITNEY GRISWOLD	WILLIAM ZECKENDORF	ARTHUR R. BURNS
HIDEKI YUKAWA	FRANK BURNET	HALIDE ADIVAR

NEW FRONTIERS
OF KNOWLEDGE

A Symposium by
Distinguished Writers,
Notable Scholars
& Public Figures

Public Affairs Press, Washington, D. C.

"The history of America is a history of frontiers—each frontier a challenge.

'We had our geographical frontiers, which were pushed farther and farther back by the men who opened up the continent. As a nation of small farmers and small shops, we had our economic frontiers. We were a nation of political frontiersmen. Franklin, Washington, Jefferson, Lincoln dared to think new thoughts about the way men should govern themselves, the institutions and the procedures they should set up. They devised a system that has stood the test of time. With mankind entering a new era, we face new frontiers of knowledge.

"These new frontiers challenge us to dare more, to do more, to go forward on a broader front. We believe that humanity makes progress with the forward thrust of the frontiers of knowledge—and we believe as well that the task is a truly international one, transcending national boundaries and calling forth the utmost in cooperation.

"This is the spirit that moved the Voice of America to invite honored and authoritative voices from many lands to share its microphones in a common effort with some of our own leading thinkers. There is likely to be both agreement and difference in the course of this unique undertaking. But honest difference discloses new frontiers too, and so I am glad to welcome our guest participants and thank them for their thoughtful contributions."

PRESIDENT DWIGHT D. EISENHOWER

Book copyright, 1957, by Public Affairs Press
419 New Jersey Ave., S.E., Washington 3, D.C.

Printed in the United States of America
Library of Congress Catalog Card No. 57-12453

INTRODUCTION

No modern King Canute behind an iron curtain could hold back the great waves of truth in this powerful collection of statements on the future of the world. The words and concepts are as fundamental as life and death. And they provide well-grounded hope for a better life of peace and freedom.

The Voice of America speaks at its best in these pages, giving tongue to the considered views of leading thinkers among the free men of many nations. It is obvious that no planner in Washington attempted to prescribe the things said in this series—these are clearly the diversified statements of men accustomed to the air of freedom. They could not have been written under regimentation.

"We are convinced that humanity is on the threshold of a new age with potentialties which challenge the imagination," declared Theodore C. Streibert when, as Director of the U. S. Information Agency, he invited the participation of the distinguished people quoted here. "The discovery of ways to release and control atomic energy is but the scientific manifestation of an era of social, political and spiritual change. The new age confronts the world with new problems and responsibilities as well as prospects. We believe the wisdom and vision of the best minds of the age can contribute to a better understanding of the hopes of humanity during the second half of this century."

One of the things which makes me proud to be an alumnus of the international information organization is the steady contribution it has made to the expansion of intellectual frontiers, in spite of the ups and downs brought by world events and changing American politics. The book program and the exchange of persons programs have accomplished most; but all elements of the operation have played a part, and in the series here presented, the radio arm leads the rest.

It is contributions like this symposium, and the straight factual reporting of news, that give the Voice of America its reputation for a degree of political and intellectual honesty not always present in the emanations from the international broadcasting services of certain other nations.

It is worth a moment's pause here to consider how it happens that programs of such importance yet of a controversial nature come forth from the Voice. The answer lies in great measure in that solid core of unsung public servants who have kept the policy and the machinery of the information organization on a fundamentally sound track through good times and bad over the past dozen years. The occasional tributes paid to the organization are usually accorded top officers who come and go—but great praise belongs to able careerists who will always insure that the voices of free intelligence are heard.

REED HARRIS

PUBLISHER'S PREFACE

Although this book is based upon a series of talks broadcast throughout the world by the United States Information Agency, it is not, strictly speaking, an official publication. It was prepared entirely at the initiative of the publisher with the cooperation of USIA and of the various participants in the symposium.

Most of the statements appearing herein follow closely the texts of the original papers. However, a number have been changed by the authors so as to bring their copy up to date or into line with their latest thinking. Lee de Forest, for example, decided to omit his original prediction that a man-made moon-voyage would never occur. "In recent months," he explained in a letter of May 14, 1957, "such great advances have been made in rockets and guided missiles that I have come to the conclusion that within the next fifty years a projectile may possibly succeed in reaching the moon, but this will be a manless vehicle, unless per-chance some enthusiast chooses the distinction of being the first mortal to rest his bones on the moon's surface. I am unable to conceive the possibility of a return voyage. Considering my change of view on this subject, I prefer to delete from my address my statement . . . that a man-made moon voyage will never occur." For the sake of the record it should also be added that Dr. Jung's statement is a simplified version of a much longer and more technical paper which did not lend itself easily to shortwave radio broadcasting.

Needless to say, the views expressed herein are solely those of the contributors and do not reflect official policies of the USIA. Responsibility for many of the titles belongs with the publisher; the phrasing used is necessarily designed to merely suggest the distinctive nature and scope of each article. Incidentally, the original title of the symposium, "Frontiers of Knowledge," is not used because a recent but wholly different book has this title.

So many persons contributed to the success of the symposium that it is impossible to list all their names, but none deserves more credit in this connection than Leonard Reed, special projects editor of the Voice of America staff. To Arthur Larson, Director of USIA, the publisher is indebted for gracious cooperation that made this book possible. Walter L. Smith and Walter Wheeler were exceedingly helpful in getting the manuscript and proofs ready for publication.

M. B. Schnapper, Editor

CONTENTS

The Future of Freedom

CHARLES MALIK

The nation will remain as a basic political concept, but sovereignty is already undergoing fundamental transformation. In this transformation the independent and sovereign nation will of course remain free to decide what it pleases, but the increasingly interdependent world will bring to bear upon national decision many more limiting factors than it did in the past. Wise leadership will have to take these factors into account; the alternative is chronic instability.

Thus internationalism will be modulated, among other things, by interculturalism. Already it is evident that there are six or seven cultures in the world which move and act each more or less as a bloc in international relations. The ultimate problem is not therefore political; it is rather how these distinct, and at times antagonistic, world views can live together in peace. The political is often the instrument, more or less disguised, of the cultural. Peaceful and productive international relations require an order of freedom, tolerance, mutual respect. They also require clear separation of realms—namely, the natural, human, almost unlimited realm where common action is both possible and necessary, and the special realm of ultimate convictions where each must feel secure under the protection of the order of freedom and respect. There should be a common, human, natural realm, or else there is utter despair of reason.

It is the historical duty of those who understand these things to press and work for this order of freedom. Considering that the world has had some history of a few thousand years in which its

---

A leading spokesman of the Arab world, Dr. Malik has played an important role in post-war international diplomacy. He has been the Lebanese Ambassador to the United States and to the United Nations. At the present time he is Lebanon's Minister for Foreign Affairs and National Education.

various parts developed more or less independently, a culturally pluralistic world becomes an absolute necessity in a physically unified world. Pluralistic freedom, then, is not the special philosophy of this or that nation or culture or group of nations or cultures; it is an absolute, immediate historical necessity. If it happens also to coincide with the basic idea of some cultures, then these cultures must be thankful that their ultimate principle has anticipated the present necessities of history. That is their deepest source of strength, to which they cannot prove unfaithful.

Nor is "coexistence" the invention of this or that ideology. It is a welcome, if perhaps also belated, recognition of the order of freedom. It is another term for the historical necessity of which we have spoken, whether or not Communism had ever existed. Properly understood and genuinely held, it is a triumph for the idea of freedom. Freedom must exploit this triumph in its own interests, which, as we have seen, are the interests of peace.

But there are two senses to freedom: freedom of the group and freedom of the individual. There is freedom of the group or culture or nation to be itself vis-a-vis other groups or nations or cultures; and there is freedom of the individual to seek and know and be in the truth. The latter alone is what is meant by freedom of thought and conscience. These two freedoms need not conflict with each other, and in a genuine order of freedom they would not; but in fact they do. In the majority of cases today, the quest or exercise of group freedom entails, either as a matter of principle or as a matter of necessity, the curtailment of individual freedom. People want national or class or cultural freedom, but they will not concede freedom to the individual to hold different views on fundamental matters from what the culture or the class or the nation does. They thus betray a static conception of the character of their group, not knowing that group character can, does and, at times, must change—especially in a nonstatic age—provided human dignity is thereby either enhanced or at least undiminished. They subordinate the individual to the group, not knowing that the group has no eternal destiny, whereas, the individual human soul is immortal. Groups, all groups, exist in the service of this soul.

How to reconcile group freedom to individual freedom is one of the most important challenges facing the world in the second half of this century. The Universal Declaration of Human Rights is helpful in meeting this challenge. It works out in measured terms a balanced view of the rightful claims of both types of freedoms; it enjoys enormous prestige, having been most carefully elaborated by the United Nations and adopted without a single dissenting vote; and it has already been significantly energized throughout the world. But there will never be any genuine reconciliation in the idea of freedom, any real peace in the order of freedom, if believers in individual freedom are going, for any reason whatsoever, to falter or faint in their persuasion. Group freedom is a primitive, robust, massive thing; it will always naturally assert itself; it hardly needs any special protection. It is individual freedom that is relatively new and fragile, and that therefore requires every possible tender care. The ultimate problem of the twentieth century is neither war nor peace, neither justice nor liberation, neither security nor the self-determination of peoples, neither Asia and Africa nor the place of America and Russia in the modern world; much as all these are real and insistent issues. The ultimate problem with which we have to wrestle is whether under the pressure of group, nation, culture and the machine, some remnant of man, of the individual human person, can still be saved. It is man who is in peril and not the society of man. And should those who believe in man themselves succumb to these pressures, man will be lost.

This does not mean—it cannot mean—that the objective economic, social, cultural and political rights are not real and should not be promoted and observed. My point is that these are so conspicuous and vociferous today, so ably advocated and thunderously agitated for, that there can be no possibility that they will not be attended to. The real danger is that in the process man will be lost, leaving behind him only a drab, mechanical array of cultures and groups soullessly pitted against one another, without inner personal freedom and therefore without hope and without joy. Never was it more necessary to stress, to bring and point out, to insist upon, the personal, the inner, the human, the free, *at the same time* that the material and social and cultural clamor for attention, than it is today. Otherwise the latter could easily end by swallowing up and abolishing the former, and the most precious thing in man, the freedom of his mind and conscience, will have gone. And when freedom is gone and the joy and being of the spirit is choked, all the technology and "culture" and national glory and material well-being in the world will avail man nothing.

The vistas opened up by the harnessing of atomic energy are tremendous. Already the effects of this discovery—through the properties of radioactive isotopes—upon industry, agriculture and medicine are revolutionizing these sciences and techniques. When the plentiful power released by the atom is put at the service of man, especially in the production of food and clothes from the sea (and this will probably come about in the second half of this century), one can clearly imagine the further incredible revolution the atom will effect for the overpopulated regions of the world. Think of the difference this will make to the arid areas of the Middle East alone. There is every reason to believe that science and technology, as they are developing today, can solve every material problem facing mankind.

This is saying a great deal; but it is not saying enough. People will still quarrel and hate one another, they will still indulge in personal, cultural and national pride, and they will still make one another's life miserable, even if, perhaps just when, all their material needs and even wants are fulfilled. The basic problem therefore is not material, although we cannot be grateful enough that science is well on the way to solving this. The basic problem is political, intellectual and spiritual. It is only as adequate leadership shall arise in these fields that we can truthfully look with confidence to the future. The scientists and technologists have magnificently lived up to their promise; it remains for these others to rise to the challenge.

Political leadership means the highest possible statesmanship whereby the ultimate international and intercultural issues today are firmly grasped and adjusted. This requires profound thought, conviction and knowledge, and a determination to take the initiative in the establishment of the order of freedom.

Intellectual leadership means philosophy in the deepest sense of the term, namely, the realization of the highest possible human wisdom. The most decisive battles, whether before or after an atomic holocaust, will be fought on the field of fundamental ideas. Only those who have the adequate, true, universal, generic ideas, and who have the conviction and courage to proclaim them, shall win.

But politics and philosophy stand under the judgment of God. It may be that God still wants to chasten the world in ways that we do not now comprehend. It may be that all of us, with all our wisdom, deserve this chastening. I believe that final hope comes from a life of prayer and simple trust in God. His will is more important than ours.

Survival in an Age of Technology

JOHN VON NEUMANN

The great globe we call earth is in a rapidly maturing crisis, which has to do with technology.

The industrial revolution consisted of making available more and cheaper energy, more and easier controls of human actions and reactions, and more and faster communications. The effect of the increased speed of technological processes was to enlarge the size of political, economic and cultural units—and to increase the danger of collision among nations, among economies, among cultures.

Technological evolution is still accelerating. Technologies are always constructive and beneficial, directly or indirectly. Yet their consequences tend to increase instability. In the military-political sphere, for example, the enormous destructive potential which large nations can harness affords little chance of a purely passive equilibrium such as represented by the old-time "balance of power."

Let us look at certain aspects of continuing technological evolution. First of all, there is a rapidly expanding supply of energy. The most significant event affecting energy is the advent of nuclear power. What massive transmutation of elements will do to technology in general is hard to imagine, but the effects will be radical indeed.

Secondly, and also likely to evolve fast—quite apart from nuclear evolution—is automation. Machines containing up to 10,000 vacuum tubes now operate faultlessly over long periods, performing many millions of regulated, preplanned actions per second. It is to be expected that the considerably elaborated newer machines now becoming increasingly available will have increasing effect on industrial efficiency.

Let us now consider a third aspect of technological advance—a thoroughly "abnormal" industry: the control of weather, or of climate. Our knowledge of the dynamics and the controlling processes in the atmosphere is rapidly approaching a level that will probably make possible, in a few decades, intervention in atmospheric and climatic matters. It will probably unfold on a scale difficult to imagine at present. There is little doubt one could intervene on any desired scale, and ultimately achieve rather fantastic effects. What power over our environment, over all nature, is implied! Measures taken in the Arctic may control the weather in temperate regions, or measures in one temperate region critically affect another, one quarter around the globe. All this will merge each nation's affairs with those of every other, more thoroughly than the threat of a nuclear or any other war may already have done.

Such developments as free energy, greater automation, improved communications, partial or total climate control, have certain common traits:

First, although all are intrinsically useful, they can lend themselves to destruction. And second, there is in most of these developments a trend toward affecting the earth as a whole. There is an intrinsic conflict with geography and institutions based thereon as understood today. This is the maturing crisis of technology.

What kind of action does this situation call for? Whatever one feels inclined to do, one decisive trait must be considered: the very techniques that create the dangers and the instabilities are in themselves useful.

In looking for a solution, it is well to exclude one pseudo-solution at the start. The crisis will not be resolved by inhibiting this or that apparently particularly obnoxious form of technology. Prohibition of invention and development is contrary to the whole ethos of the industrial age. It is irreconcilable with a major mode of intellectuality as our age understands it.

A much more satisfactory solution than technological prohibition would be eliminating war as "a means of national policy." But whether practical considerations will suffice to restrain the human species is dubious, since the past record is so spotty. True, this time the danger of destruction seems to be real rather than apparent, but there is no guarantee that a real danger can control human actions better than such convincing appearances of danger as we've seen in the past.

What safeguard remains? Under present conditions it is unreasonable to expect a novel cure-all. For progress is no cure. The only safety possible is relative, and it lies in an intelligent exercise of day-to-day judgment.

Present awful possibilities of nuclear warfare may give way to others even more awful. Atfer global climate control becomes possible, perhaps all our present involvements will seem simple. We should not deceive ourselves; once such possibilities become actual, they will be exploited. It will therefore be necessary to develop suitable new political forms and procedures. All experience shows that even smaller technological changes than those now in the cards profoundly transform political and social relationships. Experience also shows that these transformations are not *a priori* predictable and that most contemporary "first guesses" concerning them are wrong. For all these reasons, one should take neither present difficulties nor presently proposed reforms too seriously.

The one solid fact is that the difficulties are due to an evolution that, while useful and constructive, is also dangerous. Can we produce the required adjustments with the necessary speed? The most hopeful answer is that the human species has been subjected to similar tests before and seems to have a congenital ability to come through after varying amounts of trouble. To ask in advance for a complete recipe would be unreasonable. We can specify only the human qualities required: patience, flexibility, intelligence.

Education for the Future

RAMASWAMI AIYAR

Every age presents a new challenge to humanity, but the challenge of the present epoch is perhaps the most spectacular and fateful. Past conceptions of space and time, matter and life have been transformed. The infinitely great and the infinitesimally minute components of the Universe are discovered to be reservoirs of ever-functioning and ever-changing energy convertible alike to beneficent and destructive uses. The humble, yet resolute, enquirer perceives, at every turn, the workings of an inflexible rhythmic and eternal law and thus acquires a truly spiritual sense of adventure and wonder. All the same, the basic mystery of Existence stays unresolved.

Truly envisaged, the science of today and tomorrow should bring to us the same revulsion from narrowness, selfish regimentation, cruelty and oppression and the same insistence on creative activity, harmony and tolerance that ought to characterise a well-ordered social and religious training. There is, thus, no need to separate the scientific from the humanitarian and spiritual aims of education.

What shall be the future of education? In this age of specialized applications of science and technology, is man to become a thinking automaton? Shall he be simply dexterous in the fashioning of every new gadget catering to his creature comforts and in the devising of newer and newer apparatus and machines with infinite powers of wholesale destruction almost changing the face of nature? Or, in the alternative, will mankind subordinate every

---

One of India's most distinguished educators, Dr. Aiyar has written exten-
sively on political, economic and religious problems. He played a promi-
nent role in negotiations with Great Britain for India's independence and
was at one time the Secretary of the National Congress Party. At the
present time he is Vice-Chancellor of the Benares Hindu University.

consideration to the creation of an environment of physical and
economic well-being, of mental alertness and of spiritual poise?
And will he, by this emphasis, produce a self-reliant and self-
expressive personality, full of tolerance but determined to resist
regimentation, aggression and all the denials of legitimate freedom? Surely, the answer can only be in favor of the latter alternative.

The emergence of such an alternative depends in the main on
the right type of education. The child will begin to learn through
play and through a life lived in intimate contact with his fellow-
beings and nature. Such a child will be taught to observe and to
cherish plant, bird and animal without wishing to seize or to
destroy. Discipline will be directive but imperceptible, and the
questioning spirit of the child will be responded to and not re-
buked or evaded. The cultivation of an appreciation of the beautiful and appropriate in Nature, Art and Story will be the task
of the unobtrusive teacher who, from the beginning, will instill
ideas of neighbourliness and helpfulness.

The next period of adolescence will enable the growing boy
and girl to learn the habits of accurate and logical thinking. He
will acquire some skill or craft or art involving the harmonious
cooperation of the hand, the eye, the ear and the brain. The
adolescent will obtain a grounding in the basic knowledge relating
to the organic and inorganic world, and will train his emotional
reactions to respond to the calls of beauty, truth and justice. All
prejudice — racial, communal or social — should be eradicated.
And at the end of the secondary stage in education the young boy
or girl should be able to turn his or her hand to some art, craft
technique or skill so as to be fitted for his or her life-work. He
may then either turn to a professional, technical or other vocation
or proceed to a university or other center of higher learning. But
in either case he would have learned by this time to distinguish the
specious argument from the true, to differentiate between the beautiful and the merely meretricious or pretentious, and to be capable
of appreciating and being moved by the right type of literature,
music and the arts. His memory should not be burdened with

unconnected facts but his training should enable him to know where to look for and how to utilize knowledge and wisdom.

To those who are drawn towards higher learning or research, the universities and research institutions will impart in just proportion the disciplines of the humanities and the sciences. The students wll not be the reluctant listeners of set lectures and witnesses of formalized experiments. Rather, they will be self-reliant disciples of wise instructors and co-participants with them in the exploration of the frontiers of art and science. From first to last the emphasis of education should be on the unhesitating pursuit of truth and the eschewal of all that is petty, illogical, false or fallacious. Science, in its multiform shapes, is bound increasingly to engage the attention of the student of the future, but true education will teach him the limitations and the temptations and perils of science. Ultimately, the man and the woman of the future has to be educated to realize that what counts, in the long run, is the preservation and the unfoldment of human personality. Our obligation is to harmonize the fullest self-expression with a tolerance which knows and will recognize no barriers amongst creeds and races and nations. It is to develop a sense of justice which will neutralize cruelty and aggressiveness and will work for reconciliation, for the "Samavaya" of Asoka — namely, the spirit of live and let live for which all the sages of our race have pleaded.

Such results are not possible of achievement unless our religions, divorced from dogma or narrowing creeds and separatisms, become dynamically regulating factors working for peace and concord. Nor are they possible unless science, along with its stimulation of the critical and enquiring faculties, also recognizes its inevitable limitations and boundaries—and thus becomes the ally of that religious spirit which is founded on humility, wonder and reverence.

Thus shall we implement the Vedic precept, "let us come together, let us discuss in harmony and let us be reconciled in spirit" —and thus will come about the efflorescence of human personality which is the problem and the aim of all education.

New Horizons of Science

PERCY BRIDGMAN

It is, I think, generally accepted that the one characteristic which dramatically distinguishes the contemporary world from all the eras of the past is the advanced stage of technological development. As a consequence, the daily life of every inhabitant of this globe is in process of drastic transformation. This is too obvious to demand detailed proof. It would appear, however, that we are only at the beginning, and that we have every right to anticipate future developments which will have even greater impact on our daily life. Control of the sub-atomic world holds in promise not only such things as abundant power — but perhaps also, in the dimmer future, controlled transmutation of the elements and the laying of the specter of the exhaustion of our supply of the useful metals. Biological possibilities are even more exciting. A safe and cheap contraceptive will provide the desperately needed means of population control. The problem of the synthesis of food from inorganic sources will doubtless ultimately be solved, and there are even indications that the synthesis in the laboratory of the living from the non-living is not an impossibility.

All such technological advances rest on a scientific foundation and imply the prior development of pure science. In the popular mind the impact of science on our daily life, through technology, is doubtless the most important characteristic of science; indeed, science is often identified with its technological consequences. Nevertheless, I venture to suggest that the most important impact of science is not in its transformation of the external conditions of

---

Scientist as well as philosopher, Dr. Bridgman has made notable contributions in both fields. For his work on the properties of substances under very high pressures he was awarded the Nobel Prize in 1946. His research has resulted in techniques for greatly increasing the strength of metals. After forty years of teaching and study at Harvard University he recently retired from the faculty of that distinguished institution.

our daily living, but in something much deeper, namely in our complete world outlook. The modern amenities of daily life can be accepted without any drastic change in world outlook — the housewife who orders a month's supply of food by telephone and puts it in the deep freeze need not have a world outlook greatly different from her mother, who trudged to market on foot and hurried to eat her purchase before it spoiled.

The change in world outlook forced on us by science is in process of taking place and is by no means yet complete; in fact, we cannot now even guess what the eventual outcome will be. Looking back to the past, we can distinguish various important episodes in a transformation that is occurring all the time. The transformation doubtless began at least as far back as the Greeks, but to make our point we need not go further back than Sir Isaac Newton, whose laws of motion and the application of the universal inverse square law of gravitation to the motion of the heavenly bodies presented the concept of an orderly world, and inspired philosophical reactions which went as far afield as to mold the political philosophy of the American founding fathers, and that of the English and French philosophers from whom they learned. A second dramatic episode was the proof of organic evolution by Darwin, in consequence of which man was displaced from his supposed unique place in the biological scheme, no less effectively than the earth had been displaced from its central position in the cosmos by Newton. The implications of the insights of Newton and Darwin have by now been pretty well assimilated into the thinking of all the modern world, but this assimilation has not always been easy and has taken time. Other insights resulting from later scientific developments have not yet been assimilated, and in fact the full implications of some of the most recent of them are probably not yet appreciated by most scientists themselves.

After Darwin's theory of evolution, perhaps the most important change in world outlook forced by scientific discovery arose from the shocking experience of physicists with relativity and quantum theory. New discoveries in the realm of high velocities and the realm of the very small showed that our former concepts were no longer valid, concepts which we had thought were compelled by inner logical necessity. The new insight — that when we extend the frontiers of our experience we must expect to find new things which could not even have been anticipated — has, I think, been pretty well assimilated into the thinking of the scientist. But it has not, I am sure, yet been assimilated into the thinking of everyday life. In the political arena we are still trying to force old concepts, such as rights and duties, to do service under a range of conditions immensely wider than the range in which the concepts arose.

The insights afforded by relativity and quantum theory have to do primarily with the way we think, but in only a somewhat restricted way. More recent developments, I believe, are going to compel a much more drastic revision of attitude toward all aspects of intellectual activity. These developments are suggested by such catch words as "cybernetics", "information theory", "Gödel's theorem", "theory of perception". In consequence of them we are beginning to get some insight into the way the brain works and are on the road to understanding the nature of thought. Human thinking and all it involves is in process of taking its place among the natural biological processes, just as the human animal, after Darwin, took its place with the rest of the animal kingdom. And because thinking is done with the brain, which is a nervous system, any possible thought must be subject to the limitations imposed by the system which produces it. It is my personal conviction that we do not yet know how to use our minds, and that all human thinking since the beginning of thought has been ignoring inexorable limitations. When we find what the limitations are I believe that our philosophy, religion, and politics will be revolutionized.

Finally, a word about the future place of science and scientist in society. At present, in spite of all the technological amenities, there is a widespread and often ill-concealed animosity toward science and scientists. The existence of this animosity I think should not be minimized, as it often is, but it must be clearly recognized that there is here a fundamental antagonism. Science is a way of life, in addition to everything else that it is, and this way of life is temperamentally uncongenial to perhaps the majority of people. More than anything else, the scientist wants to know and understand, merely for the sake of understanding and with no ulterior purpose, even if what he finds is unpleasant. Most people prefer the philosophy that "What you don't know can't hurt you", and are willing to ignore unpleasant facts as far as they can. The scientist regards unwillingness to know the facts as the supreme immorality. Furthermore, most scientists utterly repudiate the thesis of too many that the most important function of science is to serve the State. One of the tasks of the society of the future is to find a basis for peaceful coexistence of the scientific and the non-scientific temperaments. It is an important problem, because scientists are becoming more numerous and our whole culture increasingly demands them. Furthermore, it should be a problem that is capable of solution, because society in the past has solved a somewhat similar problem, the problem of finding how to live peacefully with its artists.

The Price of War and Peace

BENJAMIN CARRION

Force and violence bring forth nothing. That is the belief of men of goodwill everywhere. This belief was underscored recently by President Eisenhower, when he promised to take every honorable measure to promote the peaceful cooperation of the countries of the world.

The great French poet, Paul Fort, described man's hope of peace in these words: "If only to all men," he wrote, "were given the reality of the supreme hope, that which the gospel commands, that they live in peace and love, employing all the moral and spiritual forces of man, building our world enriched and fertile for our children, and a peace to receive our bones when Mother Earth calls us . . ."

The poignance of man's age-old quest for peace is told in a grim anecdote of old Greece. It is said that the warrior, Alcibiades, at the arch of the temple in Athens, asked Socrates, "What is peace, master?" After meditating a few minutes, the old philosopher replied: "Peace is the time when the children bury their parents." Alcibiades, a bit taken back by the response, determinedly inquired, "And what is war, master?" The wise man quickly answered, "War is the time when the parents bury their children."

The impact of Socrates' response is profound. It goes to the roots of how alien is war to human nature. War alters the path of generations. It weakens the species of human beings, as it takes to the grave the most vigorous, the strongest force—youth. And if that was true in the time of the Greeks, how much more true is it in this epoch of mighty advances in weapons of death,

As president of the Casa de la Cultura in Quito, Dr. Carrión has contributed much to the cultural advances of Ecuador. He directs the activities of his country's national art museum, several educational institutions, two radio stations, and various cultural activities.

weapons which make war a diabolic means of destroying every-thing—man, woman and child; cities of treasure, works of art, libraries, museums, beautiful buildings. The works of civiliza-tion which took not only centuries but milleniums to build can be destroyed in a few hours if man's intelligence is to be used for destruction. All of our civilization—our Christian teaching, the voice that tells man, "Love thy neighbor"—all are menaced by the blind and dark forces of ignorance.

But if war is born in the minds of men, then it is in the minds of men that we must combat war. And it follows that combatting war in the minds of men is an increasing responsibility for men of culture, writers, teachers, newspapermen, philosophers and artists. They must employ all the resources of their intelligence, all the resources of science, to consolidate the spirit of peace, to educate men, to help men work constructively rather than toward annihilation.

Certainly all statesmen of stature believe that science should direct its work toward the peaceful use of atomic energy. The force of the atom, whose power is hardly known, is a force which could transform the world. It would offer everybody, the rich and the poor, more conveniences and less injustice. The natural wealth of today is enjoyed by only the fortunate few. But it could enter the homes of the many, in the form of utensils, tools, machinery. Thus would equality be extended, more generously, more effec-tively.

And then the atomic era that we regard with fear and mistrust would be a real blessing for the entire family. Confusion and fear would disappear in the common collaboration for universal welfare. Let us face the future with confidence that the tre-mendous force which has been discovered will be directed not toward death, but toward life.

Outlook for Philosophy

SIDNEY HOOK

Philosophy in the modern world plays an humble role. Gone are the days when, as queen of the sciences or even as handmaiden of theology, philosophy laid down the laws of Being or tried to decipher the grammar of eternity. Today philosophy in the Anglo-American tradition spends a great deal of time trying to justify its existence as a special subject matter or discipline. Those who look to philosophy for guidance are more likely to find philosophers discussing what it means for someone or something to be a guide, and other semantic questions, than any concrete recommendations for a way of life.

And up to a point this is as it should be. For if the philosopher is considered as Plato viewed him, as a spectator of all time and existence, then his function has been adequately taken over by the scientist. For it is the scientist, most broadly conceived, who gives us reliable knowledge about the nature of nature, the nature of society, and the nature of man. The philosopher who believes he was avenues to knowledge other than the methods of hypothetical-experimental science—who believes that faith can pronounce on matters of fact, or that the findings of inquiry must be corrected by a party line or church line lest it go astray—is, I believe, deluding himself and others. As I read the claims that have been made to knowledge, I conclude that there is no knowledge except scientific knowledge. This last statement may be considered as a truth about human knowledge. Or it may be considered as a resolution to use the term "knowledge" only for beliefs which are based on adequate, empirically verifiable evidence.

Of what use then is philosophy? Is the philosopher anything

Noted scholar and writer, Professor Hook is Chairman of the Department of Philosophy of New York University. As a founder and leading member of the Congress for Cultural Freedom, he has actively promoted the defense of intellectual liberty.

else than a logician or an analyst of other men's words, a gram-
marian of the rules of scientific inquiry?   Of course one can regard the philosopher as a poet or dramatist or a seer of visions.
But then one must admit that as a poet or artist he writes dull
prose.

Nonetheless there is a legitimate role which philosophy can
play today.   This role is not an imitation of natural science nor
an invitation to salvation.   And it is a role which was already
recognized by Socrates, the father of the grand tradition in Western philosophy, and stressed by John Dewey, the great American
philosopher and educator who died just a few years ago.   It pro-
claims that philosophy is a quest for wisdom.   What is wisdom?
Wisdom is often contrasted with knowledge but this is a mistake.
For wisdom is itself a *kind* or *species* of knowledge.   It is knowledge of the nature, growth, and destiny of human *values*.   We
look to the philosopher not to tell us about the nature of steel,
chalk, water; corporations, cities, division of labor; after-images
and neuroses.   This is the scientist's work. We look to the philosopher to tell us about the most satisfying uses to which our knowledge of things is to be put.   We look to him to tell us about the
most desirable ways in which social institutions could be organized
in order to liberate the greatest possibilities of individual growth.
We look to him to tell us which patterns of human experience are
more likely to give us both serenity and joy, adventure and safe
return, security and freedom.

Philosophy, then, is a form of criticism and evaluation, but a
criticism and evaluation of a certain kind.   It is a criticism and
evaluation of our value judgments as these concern the great and
momentous issues of life and death.   It differs from science not
so much by the spirit and nature of its inquiry—for although techniques differ in various fields the underlying pattern of sound
thinking is everywhere the same—but in its subject matter. Philosophy is concerned with human values and the conflict of values
in order to discover which values reflect the greatest wisdom, and
are therefore the most desirable.

This is impossible, say some philosophers.   Scientific method or intelligence can only give us knowledge about means but not about ends. It can tell us what to do in order to kill or to avoid being killed, but it can never tell us whether we should or should not kill. We can have knowledge or be wise about means but never about ends. David Hume said substantially the same thing when he maintained that intelligence is and ought to be the slave of the passions.

If we cannot be wise about human ends, then any end chosen would be reasonable as any other. But the truth is that we do not believe that all ends are equally valid or desirable. We argue about ends, we judge them in the light of alternatives, we test them by consequences, we appraise their worth in terms of the probable costs of achieving them and not achieving others. Our passions are always present but intelligent inquiry enables us to modify our passions, find substitute equivalents for them, and in this way *govern* them instead of being blindly enslaved to them.

Of course we can only agree about ends if we also agree about the desirable consequences. But the question of what constitutes desirable consequences is an open question which cannot be settled in advance. It can be decided only from case to case.

Philosophy as a quest for wisdom uses all the relevant methods of scientific inquiry to resolve disagreements in attitude and judgment, and to answer the questions: what is of more worth? and what should we do? Philosophy's work is therefore never done because human conflicts inescapably arise in a world of finite resources and indefinite, if not infinite, desires and ambitions.

What the ordinary man does unconsciously and episodically, the philosopher does consciously and systematically. To do his work well the philosopher cannot commune with eternity, but must concern himself with the world of men, of passion and conflict, and seek to bring the order of understanding and fruitful resolution to the human community.

At its best, philosophy offers, in addition to understanding, new visions, new meanings, new idioms and modes of examining problems and ways of looking at man in the world. It cannot become a weapon of a nation, a class, a party or faction without narrowing its conception of intelligence and of man.

Committed to constant inquiry, the true philosopher like the true scientist is or should be perpetually at war against superstition, against intellectual oppression, against any dogma or organization which would trammel the free play of criticism and imagination. Whatever else true philosophers differ about, however variant their credos, however different their imagination and insight, I propose to them this conception of philosophy—namely, the untrammeled quest for wisdom—as the least common denominator of their calling. It is this conception which—to adapt a phrase of Henri Bergson—will make men of thought more willing to act, and men of action more thoughtful.

The Challenge of Our Era

ARNOLD TOYNBEE

What, in my view, are the major conflicts or problems with which mankind will have to wrestle during the second half of this twentieth century? Everyone answers this dark question at his peril. But it would be still more perilous to leave it unanswered and drift forward into the future with one's eyes shut.

I will start with the most hazardous answer of all. In my expectation, the major conflict ahead of us does not seem likely to take the form of a third world war fought with atomic weapons. Our new weapons would annihilate combatants and civilians alike, and this on both sides impartially; and these are two such revolutionary changes in the traditional presuppositions of the institution of war that I should not be surprised if the result were to be the abolition of war instead of the self-annihilation of the human race. This would open up new and happier prospects for mankind, considering that, in the past, war has usually been the immediate cause of the declines and falls of civilizations. All the same, the abolition of war cannot be expected to bring with it the abolition of tension, strife, and trouble. These evils were not abolished by the abolition of slavery that was achieved in the nineteenth cenutry. They are the perennial fruits of the 'Original Sin' which is inborn in human nature.

The abolition of war, working in combination with the lowering of the death rate through our recent vast improvements in public hygiene, is going to raise, in an acute form, the problem of population that was foreseen by Malthus more than a century and a half ago. Is mankind going to rid itself of two of its three traditional scourges—war and pestilence—only to be done to death by

One of the honored and articulate scholars of our age, Dr. Toynbee is probably the most influential of living historians. He is best known for his ten-volume work, "A Study of History." Until 1957 he was Director of the Royal Institute of International Affairs in London.

the third scourge, famine? Surely we are not going to be so stupid as that. Yet, when we have done all that science can do to increase the world's food supply, the only way left open to us for coping with the continuing increase in population through the reduction of the death-rate will be to offset this increase by a corresponding reduction in the birth-rate; and here we come up against a problem that is a formidable one, because of its political and religious implications. The death-rate can be lowered easily and rapidly, even in a backward country, by a small staff of trained public health officers applying fairly simple measures. The birth-rate, on the other hand, can be lowered only by persuading or compelling parents to limit the size of their families. To persuade them might mean persuading them to change some of the tenets of their ancestral religion. To coerce them would mean a tyrannical interference, by the public authorities, with a man and wife's freedom to bring children into the world—a freedom which, in the past, has been respected by even the most tyrannical governments so far known to history.

Yet the problem of limiting the birth-rate will have to be faced. The alternative is starvation. And freedom from want is now being claimed as a right all over the world, even in regions where, till lately, wholesale death by famine was still being taken as a matter of course. Security and social justice are, today, the first priorities for the majority of mankind, and one of our problems is going to be that of striking a new balance between justice and freedom. There always has to be a compromise between these two desiderata, because each is inimical to the other and yet mankind cannot live without enjoying a bit of both. The maintenance of a perpetually shifting balance between freedom and justice is one of Man's permanent social problems. In the chapter of history on which we are now entering, the balance seems likely to shift in favour of justice and security at the cost of freedom—partly because, compared with security, freedom is a luxury, and partly because freedom becomes more and more dangerous as we continue to equip ourselves with more and more high-powered tools.

Yet Man cannot live without freedom on some plane of life;

and, if freedom on the economic and political planes is going to be increasingly restricted by the demand for justice and by the safety regulations of the machine-age, then human nature is sure to seek compensation by insisting on being given freedom in some other sphere. The obvious other sphere is religion, and this brings us face to face with another problem.

How is modern Man going to fill the spiritual vacuum in his soul? This vacuum has been created by the rise of modern science. Science has expelled religion in its traditional forms; yet science, by itself, is incapable of filling the void. Science has given Man an unprecedented degree of control over non-human nature, including the bodies that human souls inhabit; but science does not help Man to control himself; and self-control is always Man's most urgent and most difficult problem. It is particularly urgent today, just because our control over non-human nature has been so vastly increased. Man today is like an adolescent armed with an adult's weapons without having attained to an adult's state of mind. He will be a danger to his fellows, and still more to himself, till he grows up spiritually to match his now gigantic technological stature. But the way towards spiritual maturity runs, not through science, but through religion. I therefore expect to see twentieth-century Man set out on a quest for the recovery of religion. I believe that he will recover it. But I also believe that it will come back in forms that will be so different from the traditional forms that, at first sight, Man's new religion may hardly be recognisable.

What will be the touchstone by which we shall know that this is true religion all the same? The touchstone of religion is its capacity to deal with the problem of suffering; and our sufferings seem likely to be great in the testing time that lies ahead of us.

Hopes for a Better World

CARLOS P. ROMULO

It will depend entirely on the manner we will solve our present problems whether the generations to come will enjoy a full life or not. I need not say that it is our duty to make that life possible by making use of the advantages we have gained in our efforts to improve our standards of living. Some of these advantages are so incredible that it would be tragic to let them go to waste or otherwise misuse them. For instance, the split atom. By this discovery we have tapped the greatest source of energy we have yet known, and yet this energy may be utilized for ends other than the interests of human advancement.

It is a supreme irony that as we have advanced to a point nearest the achievement of the more abundant life, we have, at the same time, come closest to the verge of the percipice. Perhaps it would be more correct to say that we are now on the brink and may slip any tim.

Having split the atom, and having proved the efficacy of the energy thus released for the extermination of human multitudes, we have proceeded at a pace faster than sound to the perfection of bombs at least ten times as destructive as the original one dropped at Hiroshima. And not satisfied with this record, we have produced the nuclear weapon about the power of which to incinerate the human race from off the face of our planet there remains not the slightest doubt.

The immediate problem then before us is how to control the use of the stupendous energy we have just learned to produce from the atom. The present is the time to decide on this control, not the future, for there will be no future to speak of if we are

---

Author, playwright, and statesman of the Philippine Republic, General Romulo is eminently qualified to explain the Eastern mind to the West and the Western mind to the East. He is at present the Philippine Ambassador to the United States and to the United Nations Security Council.

wiped out now, as we are sure to be if the nuclear spark is ignited.

We find the most serious obstacle to agreement on control certain types of men accustomed to the uses of brute force, sadistic men who rule mililons who must remain in ignorance for the convenience of the minorities that decide for them. The tragic thing about that ignorance is the fact that those millions are not aware that they cannot possibly escape death in a nuclear war.

Thus it becomes the serious concern of free men everywhere to tear down the iron curtain that keeps so many millions ignorant or misinformed. The forces of enlightened opinion must go into action seriously to release those millions from their shackles. So many minds freed and restored to the normal function of thinking are bound to bring to an end the regimes that are responsible for keeping the nuclear weapon as an instrument for blackmail and conquest.

The crusade of enlightenment must be launched without further loss of time and to my mind the Voice of America is in the best position to lead the crusade. There will be no end to the present deadlock in the disarmament talks so long as so many millions behind the Iron Curtain are not thinking as they should, thanks to their rulers who want to perpetuate themselves in power. The crusade must help restore responsible leadership and bring back good faith to the chancelleries of the world.

I cannot think of a more plausible idea than the Eisenhower "open skies" inspection plan. For the Russian people as well as for all other peoples in the world it is just the thing to prove good faith. Concealment cannot serve any purpose except to bring about mutual destruction, for the West can disguise atomic arsenals no less successfully than the Russians. It is obvious that surprise attack could come from either side, and if it did, there is always room for retaliation. There will be no trumpets to proclaim victory, after the last flame of the holocaust has died out.

It is sad to think how successfully history has glamorized the heroes of war and laid the emphasis on armed battles and conquests. But it is not too late to change the historic course, and besides, there is no more glory in war. The gladiators of old are gone, and so are all the Light Brigades of song and story. Even the conquest of Normandy has been outmoded by the guided missile and the long-range bomber, both of which can deliver nuclear annihilation to wherever it must be inflicated. War has been reduced to terms of utter and total destruction and nothing more remains in it to aggrandize the human spirit.

If we eliminate the remaining obstacle, which is the regime of force and bad faith, there will be a chance that the international community will see the indivisible oneness of its fate in this nuclear age. It should be easy, once this situation evolved, to establish the mechanism of effective control that would ensure the use of atomic energy strictly for the ends of peace. And what should follow is the dismantling of all bomb factories and the destruction of all atomic stockpiles in the countries concerned.

The family of nations should be without armaments in the next half of this century, if it is not possible to do such a thing now. We should be laying the basis today for a complete disarmament tomorrow. So far we have turned our energies only towards *reduction* of our arms and weapons and standing armies. We have moved in the right general direction, but not exactly the right direction. If we eliminate arms altogether, leaving only the minor weapons for the strictly police end of our internal order, there is little if any chance of our venturing into war. Man will not go beyond his borders to fight with his bare fists, but if he must, so let it be.

What would happen when the so-called Big Powers are no longer such powers by virtue of the fact that they have ceased to have the infernal bombs in their arsenals or the huge standing armies within their borders? The immediate result, I think, is the liberation of enslaved men who would no longer be subdued by their armed totalitarian tyrants. There is also bound to be a complete recession from the empires of those nations that, like Russia, persist in tightening the yoke around their subjects. The messianic mission will have completely lost its *raison d'etre* because what is there to check the natural yearnings of the human spirit in dependent lands except the armed might of its oppressor?

We will have removed perhaps the last cause of friction in our human relations, when all peoples are emancipated. I see no reason why Asia and Africa should continue to be the sources of resentment and revolt, instead of the reservoir of cooperative good will. But since they are exactly what we would not want them to be—a constant threat to the peace of our time—it is vain to try not to see that a policy of force is behind it all, that while in some cases the law has been superseded by brute strength, in other cases colonial armies are making their last stand for vested interests.

It is time the dependent areas of the earth were given their political and other fundamental freedoms, instead of being isolated from the rest of the family of nations, thus depriving the world of their cooperation. It is time their peoples were being left to their own best lights to carve out their future, develop their resources as they see fit and for their benefit rather than for their alien masters, and finally take their place in our councils as our sovereign equals. Then the new order of things should spell real world collaboration on the gigantic projects of human amelioration that remain to be launched.

We should see Asia and Africa emerge from the morass into which ages of colonial imperialism have reduced them. The swamps of pestilential disease must go, the dread insects and baccilli must cease to be the constant companions of the disinherited. Man must cease to die at thirty in half of the world, while living up to eighty in the other half, the sunnier half known as the free West. Equal opportunity in international trade, such as fair price for their products, freedom from extortion by the mighty combines of Western wealth, and balanced national economies based on their own resources — these benefits, long denied them, must come to Asia and Africa in the second half of this century.

Human freedom must be complete to the last detail. All iron curtains must go, all barriers to knowledge and information must be obliterated. There should be no more subjects, but only free men; no more masters, no more slaves. Nations should be all equal, and they will be, in their solidary responsibility for the preservation of the species and its dignification before the eyes of God.

We should all be happy to leave our children to the care of an international community so conceived in the proposition that all nations have a common destiny and that all men, regardless of race, color or creed, shall enjoy equal opportunity.

Breaking the Barriers of Prejudice

MARGARET MEAD

One of the special triumphs of the human race is the way in which men have varied and yet remained one species; not like other living things continued varying until groups of distinct, isolated species were formed.   Men, in different environments, are prevailingly dark or light, tall or short, heavy or slender, always varying, always containing within each group the possibility of new variations.   Yet these varied human types can still marry and produce graceful well proportioned children.   And each temporarily isolated group—no matter how isolated, in some tangled jungle, snowy waste, or lonely island — can always be brought back into the mainstream of human history, because they are able to learn.   Throughout our history, civilizations have risen to peaks of accomplishment—groups of men working closely together with the previous high achievements of other men at their disposal have been able to add some new high point to the steadily growing storehouse of man's inventions and knowledge.   Very often it has not been their descendants who have made the next important invention, but instead the descendants of some other human group, only recently living at a far simpler level. Around the ruins of ancient palaces, almost swallowed up by jungles, simple unlettered peasant descendants may be living today—while the descendants of those who were hunters, and peasants, and fishermen, in another land when the palaces flourished, occupy the seats of learning and power today.   The torch of high achievement passes from group to group because all human groups are able—

America's foremost woman anthropologist, Dr. Mead is associated with the American Museum of Natural History. The results of her investigations of social structure and human behavior have been widely acclaimed. Among her most important books are "Coming of Age in Samoa," "Sex and Temperament in Three Primitive Societies," "Male and Female," and "New Lives for Old."

in different ways, at different periods—to take it up, hold it high and light it more brightly. What man has developed, man can learn.

This interchangeable capacity to learn, which is independent of how much one's ancestors had achieved at any moment of history, is one of the great modern discoveries. It is firmly grounded in scientific study which shows how different has been the evolutionary path taken by man, and by those living creatures who, if they are to keep an improvement in their relationship to the world must make it hereditary. These other living creatures must make it hereditary because they cannot make their experience articulate and so available both to their children and to other people's children. It is upon this tenet that Western democracy has been able to take a stand, for universal literacy, for equality of opportunity . . . not only for the new-born, but for those who have grown to manhood and womanhood lacking the skills and the knowledge of other more fortunately placed human beings. Those who believe in the capacity of all human beings to learn do not have to liquidate the adults who have learned the prejudices of a by-gone era. Because they know that adults can learn, all members of changing democratic societies can live and change.

But only just coming to be accepted is the knowledge that all racial stocks are part of one human species, with such variability, that each population contains within it the possibility of producing individuals as gifted as those who have gone before them. For thousands of years men have believed, some in good faith and some in bad, that one human group—defined by skin color, or hair form, shape of nose or shape of lips or eye—could be considered as superior to some other group. Once such a definition has been made, both groups have believed it; the group who thought themselves superior, became less human by the denial of humanity to the others; the group who accepted the definition became less human by the acceptance of a low estimate of their ability. Each time such a definition is made—from the earliest times when thousands of years ago, immigration stations were set up by kingdoms long since fallen into decay—human civilization has suffered. Institutions like slavery, peonage, caste, pogroms, concentration camps, and gas chambers have been the consequence.

We may hope, as we move into a world more firmly based on science, that an ethic which sees all men—not only those not yet born, but those already grown mature in outworn beliefs—as able to learn, will abolish the distinctions among racial groups which are based on a false belief in difference of capacity. We may also hope, and work for, a world in which it is not necessary to substitute a denial of all differences just because the differences have been wrongly interpreted. Within each racial stock, we find those with great gift, those with average gift, those with very limited abilities. Within each racial stock, and among each human group, we find the sensitive and the insensitive, the imaginative and the prosaic. In the past, a belief in inherent differences in the capacities of Caucasian, Mongolian, Negroid peoples, or between Nordic, Alpine, Mediterranean stocks, or between Jew and Gentile, have led to classifying together, as either "superior" or "inferior", the gifted and the ungifted, the perceptive and the unimaginative. By breaking down these false classifications, we may hope to substitute better ways of finding those who by nature are better suited for one fate than another, those who can make great contributions to the world store of knowledge, and those upon whom no such heavy demand should be made. When no man is put at birth automatically into a pre-judged classification, then each man—and woman—will be freer to be themselves—to reach full stature—and the whole world will benefit thereby.

Social and Cultural Change

GILBERTO FREYRE

Some years ago, Leon Daudet, the French political and social critic, wrote a book about the nineteenth century, that he called "L'stupide 19eme Siecle". He violently attacked that century as if he were attacking a person or an institution. The fact is that, through a pure convention, centuries are becoming for us the equivalents of institutions and almost the equivalents of personalities: each one viewed as if endowed with a sort of super-personality—sometimes a demoniac personality.

This is how some of us are viewing the present century. Its second half is now being considered by pessimistic interpreters of the social psychology of the twentieth century, as a sort of Mr. Hyde in relation to Dr. Jekyll. Dr. Jekyll would be the first half of the century which, by contrast with the demoniac possibilities of the second half, would be given the quality or the title of the "good" or "normal" or "virtuous" part of a split personality. In other words, and contrary to Browning: "the worst is yet to come . . ."

Have pessimists a basis for being so pessimistic in regard to the present century? Or to expect from its second half only disgrace or unhappiness for mankind? Should a century be judged as a man whose old age would be fatal exaggeration of his youthful traits?

At least from the point of view of a social analyst, the second half of the twentieth century is not to be judged but to be understood—as much as it is possible to understand an epoch by anticipation; and understood as the dramatic, but not necessarily catas-

A distinguished Brazilian social anthropologist and writer, Dr. Freyre is best known for his book "Casa Grande e Senzala" (The Big House and the Slave Hut), a trenchant social analysis which established his reputation as a scholar of the first rank. He has been a member of Brazil's Parliament and a delegate to the United Nations General Assembly.

trophic, meeting of the past with a violent future. The future probably will come to us and to our children, in the next fifty years, as a violent and sharp contrast of an atomic with a non-atomic civilization. It probably will try to become immediately present and dominant as an abnormally aggressive adolescent tries to become immediately a man: disregarding his elders to the point of being not only rude, but brutal, with them.

However, the rhythm of brutality will probably lose much of its violence, after a few years of excesses. For human experience teaches us that violent clashes between civilizations represented by different generations tend to be short. And more: they tend to be succeeded by interpenetration. Usually interpenetration means adjustment; and adjustment means, when it refers to human groups, not the elimination of tensions, but their equilibrium in a peaceful and sometimes creative, mutually complementary way.

No one of us, man or woman of the twentieth century, has the right to expect to live in a new Victorian Age: in what the Victorian age was for Europe or for the Western super-civilized peoples. For only a part of them enjoyed the pleasures and comforts of an age of stability, as active, conscious participants of that stability; while, at present, the century is being consciously or actively lived by a much larger number of human beings. Westerners have now as co-participants in their experiences as men and women of a definite century—a dynamic, unstable, socially experimental, culturally and politically adventurous century—a considerable number of Easterners; and among the Westerners themselves the number of modern, present-day men and women who are conscious of belonging to a definite century is a much larger number than the number of members of the Western civilization who were really conscious of the same fact during the nineteenth century. If history tells us that the Victorian Age was an age of comfortable stability, implying that this was an universal fact, it is because history has been written from the point of view of a part or fragment of the world: the educated segment of the West. Only now is it beginning to be really a pan-human history.

Only now the entire—or almost the entire—world is beginning

to live simultaneously in the same social and psychological time, despite differences as to how human beings should organize themselves politically, economically and socially. This new sense of human unity, brought about by a number of technological advances that already have given men a new conception of time as well as of space, will probably be intensified during the second half of the twentieth century. It will result, I think, in the growth of a pan-human conscience, especially among responsible elites everywhere. The new conscience will act as a powerful corrective to simplistic tendencies; as a corrective for viewing radical antagonisms between "East" and "West", "Collectivism" and "Individualism", as antagonisms in which these radical differences might go on indefinitely. The second half of the twentieth century may become characterized, from a sociological point of view, by a new conscience on the part of men of different parts of the world, of a more dynamic relation between space and time, through a sense of unity between the two—time and space—a conscience that until the present day has been unknown, or not realized, by human groups even within European civilization. These groups have lived in different social and psychological times, though, chronologically, in the same century. Knowledge and analysis by social scientists of this basic discrepancy is a means of bringing men and women to feel that, as contemporaries, they are, in many respects, in the same boat. To live in the same rhythm of time is to acquire the sense of belonging to a community that has no rigid geographical frontiers.

Social scientists have been, in some respects, pioneers in the rediscovery of the world as a potentially pan-human space, where differences in socio-cultural systems should not be always interpreted as inferiorities in relation to superiorities. This knowledge is beginning to give Western men a new vision of such until recently undervalued human cultures. Perhaps the second half of the present century will be marked by an almost complete recognition, by men of the so-called pure races, of the capacity and potentiality of hybrids, as carriers or creators of civilization, including Christian civilization, and also by an almost complete

recognition of the possibility of the development of such civilizations in tropical spaces by non-Europeans of dark races, or ethni-
cally mixed, whose non-Puritan or non-Western love of leisure
does not necessarily mean incapacity to work. Technology is
making possible a considerable control by men of tropical climatic
inconveniences, so as to make tropical spaces suitable to civilization in forms equivalent to—though not passively repetitive of—
the highest forms of boreal or temperate European and Anglo-
American climate; civilization is ceasing to mean only European
or Western forms of civilization, but to mean also non-European
and non-Western styles of living, characterized by complexity, re-
finement, the cultivation of art and wisdom in their highest and
subtlest expressions, such as Chinese cookery—to mention a concrete example of one of the highest human accomplishments in
art or in civilization.

The second half of the twentieth century will probably bring
an intensive acceleration to change—social change and cultural
change—among men; but this change may vary in different spaces,
with the problem of differences in social and psychological time
still an important problem to be considered and dealt with by
social analysts and by men of action.

The dependence of men of action on social analysts, for more
intelligent political and administrative measures, will probably
increase during the next fifty years, giving to the so-called "policy
making" or "policy sciences" a greater extension than at present.
More than one social analyst has suggested the convenience of
having, throughout the world, in different social and cultural
spaces, social science "weather stations" for "continuous observation, analysis and reporting."

This seems to be a real need, but its execution on a really
international scale is considerably embarrassed by the fact that
there seem still to exist rigidly national systems that would view
such social science "weather stations", to report on social time,
as undesirable. Many national leaders insist that people led by
them live in social space-times entirely of their own, without connection with other space-times; without agreeing on being ob-

served, and reported, as parts of a trans-national and pan-human, though not uniform, social system. Regarding this pan-human and trans-national system, social scientists of different countries seem to think that it has become not only a desirable but a necessary system to modern men, in a world that will have to be socially and psychologically harmonized with technological advances too great to be ignored. This effort towards harmonization will be a great task of responsible men during the second half of the twentieth century.

Tasks of Education

NATHAN PUSEY

Among the wonders of today's world are the amazing computation devices which help men to solve relatively rapidly problems too long, or impossible, to solve twenty years ago. So conspicuously successful have these machines become and so widely are they coming into use in the United States and elsewhere, that we often hear gloomy predictions that "the machine has taken over."

In a sense the machine has taken over, but the coming of the machine is just the beginning. Of itself the machine is nothing. We have always needed the mind of man, that wonderful and mysterious God-given mechanism. Mind makes it possible for man to make machines and to use them. While many of the tasks for which man's mind is inadequate are made easier by the machine, man's rational powers created the machines and man has the mental ability to determine their use. When we ask the mathematician what his new machine can do, he invariably answers that it can find the solution to any problem which can be identified and stated in logical terms. Thus we can never dispense with mind.

The analogy of man and the machine is in essence simply a statement of the educational problem throughout the world, a problem which has long been with us and will certainly be of first importance in the coming half century. How can we satisfy the demands of a dynamic and increasingly technological society for trained men and machines? How can we at the same time provide men and women with the broad background and balanced judgment to bring to bear in the world that spirit of reason on which the peace and happiness of all of us must ultimately depend?

President of Harvard University, Dr. Pusey has served in the field of education for twenty-eight years as scholar, teacher and administrator. The unviersity he presides over is the oldest in the United States

This is the task of education. In terms of the millions seeking education in those parts of the world, until now least affected by the industrial revolution, the problem of raising up both the technically trained and the reasonable men and women appears almost hopelessly immense. Yet the speed with which a beginning has been made is so exciting that one cannot help compare contemporary efforts with what was accomplished by the United States from the day of its settlement to the present. At least such comparison may give us insight into the global aspect of the task.

It took this country about a century and a half to institute a formal system of publicly supported education. Education had been a subject of concern to Americans from the beginning, but the major revolution of American education was the growth and spread of the comprehensive public high school, the purpose of which was to supply the educational need of a whole age group. Although the public-school system in this country is characteristically supported and administered at the local level, it has provided schooling for all but a fraction of the American people. Such "mass education" inevitably suffers sometimes in comparison with the European system which aims at producing a small, highly selective and carefully prepared segment of the populace. In the United States, however, we have never been willing to admit that a few only were deserving of education. Our attitude has been quite the opposite—an education is something to be set before all, so that they who most desire can have it and make use of it.

The initial stages of our educational task have now been completed. The terminal age of schooling in the United States has steadily risen, while the opportunities for high school and college education have spread throughout the 48 states. Between 1890 and 1952 the proportion of the age group attending high school shot upward from 3.8% to 65.3% and the actual numbers in high school increased from 203,000 to nearly 8,000,000. At the same time the number of high schools grew from a few thousand to almost 24,000.

Today the demand for education beyond the high school level

is constantly widening, and the current question is whether the period of formal education for all American youth is to take in the four years of college. It is only too clear when one examines the figures how far we have gone in this direction. Less than 5% of those of college age were fortunate enough to go to college in 1900. By 1930 their numbers had increased to approximately a million. Today there are more than two and a half million in college, and the statisticans predict that this number will double within the next fifteen years. It is quite possible that before the end of the century one out of every two Americans will be insisting on some sort of formal educational experience after high school.

Numbers then and the demand of numbers, have been and still are the first problems facing American education—and, indeed, education in most parts of the world. To deal with these numbers, we needed and still need teachers, and we have neither enough of them, nor enough good ones. We need an increased sense of public repsonsibility toward our educational scheme of things, an appreciation of the problems of education, of the need to pay teachers adequately and to give them a place of honor and incentive in the community. We need classrooms, laboratories, playing fields, and a host of other facilities which may aid in the educational process.

In providing educational opportunities for everyone our concern now is often directed at the serious question as to whether enough provision is made for the able and exceptional student, enough flexibility and breadth to enable the encouragement of excellence without which education for the masses would mean simply mediocrity. We in the United States took the first step in our early years by seeing that our citizen leaders were properly prepared for offices of church and state. Education in the professions became a matter of awakened interest in the middle of the nineteenth century. We have always emphasized the need for practical preparation in fields like engineering and agriculture. Yet at the same time we have found that the educated man needs most of all an ability to apply to facts that sense of values which makes possible a rational solution to human problems.

Education in the ultimate reaches depends upon the way an individual approaches knowledge—in the subtle communication between student and teacher. The creative teacher and the quality of his teaching is hardly dispensable, and one of our most serious tasks in the years ahead will be to seek out able members of every age group and encourage them to transmit to those who follow them something of the knowledge and the excitement which they in turn received from teachers who preceded them. Despite the important role which education must play in advancing the growth of the underdeveloped parts of our world—and I must emphasize how very necessary education is in the scientific and technological society which has brought great happiness and also many problems to highly developed nations—I must make one final plea that we do not allow the practical direction of education to take on too shallow a meaning. Material benefits are one thing, to be sure, but the important consideration is always the individual human mind.

We should never allow the aims of education to be defined simply in terms of the economic demands of our society. We cannot deny the importance of these demands, and we must do our best to fill them, but the higher obligation of education is to see that competence also includes the ancient virtues of loyalty, sensitivity to beauty, humility, breadth of viewpoint, patience. It is here the humanistic studies, the emphasis on people rather than subjects, and the concern for the ultimate reaches of the human spirit and for eternal truths have their part to play. It is my firm conviction that education must be the critic as much as the servant of society, for values of crucial concern to humankind are too often lost or obscured in a workaday world. In the end it is education that must save us from ourselves.

The Role of the Artist

JULES ROMAINS

Theoretically, knowledge has no limits other than those of the human mind. And experience shows that within those limits the field of discovery is practically boundless in scope and in depth.

On the other hand, there is little knowledge which cannot be used; that is, which cannot contribute to modifying man's condition. Thus, there should result a continuous—and almost infallible—improvement for humanity. Unfortunately, this astonishing capacity for knowledge developed within a being who has retained many animal characteristics. Consequently, the fruits of his knowledge are used for ends some of which are more or less reasonable—while others are criminal and confront humanity with a mounting threat of self-destruction.

These truths, banal though they may be, cannot be passed over in silence at the outset of a discussion such as this one. Otherwise we should merely indulge in a futile exchange of statements.

Each of the participants in this discussion has been invited to present, preferably, his opinion on that field of intellectual activity which is his own. This, of course, is quite natural. But we should be wary lest we thereby re-enforce a very dangerous tendency of the modern world: the increasing isolation of specialized knowledge; the sometimes absurd egocentricity of the specialists' outlook; the tighter and tighter compartmentalization of the human mind.

A priceless variety of the human species is on the verge of extinction: the person who tries to live up to the definition, and to assume the total function, of man. Let us call him *homo*

Poet, playwright and novelist, Monsieur Romains is best known for his monumental work "Men of Good Will" (Les Hommes de Bonne Volonte) —a collection of twenty-seven novels set against the historical background of the first three decades of the twentieth century. Although past seventy, he is still quite active in the literary world.

plenarius—the full man, the complete man. In the last analysis, it is for him—for this variety of the human species—that all the others work in the field of knowledge. What good is it to multiply special branches of knowledge, if these branches do not merge and do not blend into a whole—if there no longer exist minds capable of bringing them together, of establishing a proper hierarchy amongst them, of appraising them, even of measuring their potential danger?

Our future thus depends largely on the direction we will give to the education of the young. If we resign ourselves to the disappearance of *homo plenarius*, and of the part of *homo plenarius* that should exist in the specialist, we accept in advance the dislocation of the human mind, the growth of mutual misunderstanding—and finally a catastrophe which will reconcile the specialists in nothingness. That is why we should encourage those institutions which work to preserve in the world the point of view of *homo plenarius*; whether these institutions already exist, with their imperfections, like the United Nations and UNESCO; or whether they are still to be created, like that "Supreme Council of Wise Men" which I myself have never tired of recommending for many years.

The future of arts and letters is apparently conditioned by the common future of humanity. More so than in the past, when a collapse of civilization remained local and temporary. Henceforth it would be a question of total and probably final extinction. Prospects would scarcely be more cheerful if the future were to belong to a regime based on physical slavery and rigid conformity of thought. An art, a literature reduced to mere instruments of propaganda, from which freedom of thought and of inspiration have been banned as poisonous drugs, is interesting only as a semi-political, semi-propagandistic technique.

Literature and the arts, then, must concern themselves with their own fate. Can one say, with regard to them, that there is any positive hope? Those activities of the mind to which, except in primitive times, the idea of progress through the accumulation of results is alien, can at best hope that the future will not be less favorable to them than the past. Now certain fears are not inconceivable. In the fields of music and the plastic arts, an inherent cause of degradation is the need for novelty at any cost— a need from which it will surely be difficult to escape. Neither artists nor the public can be satisfied with repetition of the masterpieces of the past. And new fields of discovery are far more limited here than in the sciences. Moreover, whereas a science becomes enriched by thrusting into very specialized directions, a work of art, if it does not maintain a sufficiently broad contact with the human soul, diminishes in quality and veers toward the exceptional and the bizarre—an unmistakable sign of decadence.

Literature, so far, is less directly menaced. Either it withdraws altogether, or it must keep contact with the universality of the human soul—of which it remains the most complete expression. Moreover, the need for novelty can be more easily satisfied in literature since the subjects with which it deals—aspects of the soul and of life, both individual and collective—are in constant process of renewal themselves; this spontaneous renewal translates itself far more easily into literature than into the plastic arts.

This does not exempt literature from having to struggle against the temptation of the exceptional and the bizarre—to say nothing of the absurd.

Another theme for thought would be for the future relationship of art, including literature, and society. The main task, as we have said, is to preserve the freedom of the mind. A problem almost as important is to determine how art and literature will defend themselves against the growing effects of vulgarization, resulting both from the spread of elementary education and from the progress achieved in the techniques of its diffusion. Nor should we lose sight of the fact that the pursuit of the exceptional, of the unusual, of the absurd, is often only an easy way for the artist to escape the commonplace.

The World Americans Want

HENRY LUCE

If there is something important lacking in how the other two billion people of the world think of Americans, it is, I think, that they do not see clearly what kind of world the United States wants. This may seem strange because it is so obvious to us that we want a peaceful world, a prosperous world, preferably a democratic world. But precisely because we enjoy so many blessings, and take them so much for granted, other peoples feel that we are a little remote from *their* struggles, *their* unrealized hopes, *their* aspirations. We need to formulate our world-view, our picture of the kind of world we'd like to help to build—and having formulated that picture, we need to repeat it and explain it and illustrate it.

I shall try now to formulate a brief outline of what I conceive to be the American idea of the world we would like to *help* to build.

First, we want a world wherein every man and woman and child may worship God in the way in which he is called or taught. This means not only formal worship. We want a world where every child of God may learn about God through the faith of his fathers from his proper spiritual pastors without any let or hindrance.

All the other points follow from this because we want the kind of world God wants us to want. And if God seems to say different things through different revelations to different people—all serious revelations agree on two things. All revelations tell us that man is made for reverence, and all revelations tell us that men should live peaceably with each other. So—

Secondly, we want a world of Peace. We know that we cannot

One of the most successful publishers in American history, Mr. Luce has pioneered new ventures in magazine and pictorial journalism. He is the founder and editor of Time Incorporated—which publishes the magazines "Time", "Life", "Fortune", and "Sports Illustrated."

45

have a world without change. The first law of the universe is change—growth and decay and rebirth. No one has faced this issue more incisively than John Foster Dulles. Years ago, Mr. Dulles gave us the slogan *peaceful change*. We want a world where peaceful change is achieved by diplomacy and also by international instituitons. Peace is the work of Justice—as His Holiness The Pope frequently reminds us . . . We will hold up high the banner of Law and Lawfulness as the means toward the universal ideal of Justice.

Third, we want a world in which all men are free to seek the truth—the scientific truth, the scholarly truth, the philosophic truth—and to utter truth as they see it.

Fourth, we want a world of economic abundance. This we know is an entirely practical wish, and capable of realization in a few decades. Right now the United States can make the biggest contribution to this universal demand. But we have not yet made it clear, either to ourselves or others, how our contribution can be most effective. Abundance is not achieved by doles or handouts but by wealth-creating acivities; it is achieved not primarily by Governments but by peoples. We will make it plain to the world that we Americans have gained some special knowledge about how this is done. We by no means insist that everybody has to do it exactly our way, but we will insist as persuasively as we can that other countries shall meet us part way in creating wealth as we know it can be created.

Fifth and lastly, we want a democratic word—a world in which every tribe trends, unmistakably, to government of the people, for the people, and by the people. That is the American, the Lincolnian, statement of the proposition. Merely because the word "democracy" has been perverted and abused, we will not abandon the fight for world-wide democracy. We will assert and re-assert the faith—yes, almost the dogma—that all religious truth converges to say that democracy is the nearest proximate expression in political and social terms of the highest ideals of justice and liberty. Coming down from the abstract to the earthy—to be of the earth earthy—we will assert that the key to democracy is the ballot box. We will strive to make the ballot box sacred in every land throughout the earth.

Let then the people talk. And let them vote. Let people speak —and everywhere be spoken to.

We Americans are willing to take our chances on talk. Throughout our history we have risked it — and survived and grown. We have uttered much foolish talk in this land—all of us and our fathers. We talk, we discuss, we argue, we debate. So, as we take our stand throughout an argumentative, disputatious world, let us not be afraid to discuss, to argue, to debate with all manner of men—let us never become weary of it. Let us strive to speak with as much good sense as we can—and listen to others carefully and politely. Thus shall we really enter into the life of the world and share with others and let others share with us the whole mission of man on earth—which is to participate in the eternal dialogue of good and evil, to seek to incarnate the good in lives of mutual justice and in charity which knows no bounds.

The Long View and the Short

SALVADOR DE MADARIAGA

The twentieth century has so far witnessed two developments of an impressive magnitude: on the one hand a leap forward of the scientific and technical mastery of man over nature which dwarfs even the great achievements of the nineteenth century; on the other, a gradual simplification of the tensions of international life which has reduced the one-time turbulent world-stage to a duel between two formidable groups.

These two trends seem at first mutually independent. They are, however, but two aspects of the same phenomenon: the gradual evolution of mankind towards a full awareness of its total self in the presence of the universe. Viewed in this light, the present set of conflicts acquire a dramatic relief: mankind is being challenged by destiny. If we fail to meet this challenge, the very power of our weapons wielded by our unworthy hands, will fatally destroy us. If we realize that the era of the H-Bomb must be the era of supra-national reason, we shall enter the next stage in our evolution towards our true selves.

The signs of the times are not so far very good. The world is divided by a chasm between two ways of life, one of which amounts to a repulsive return to the ways of the worst barbarous eras; while the other, well-meaning and generous though it endeavors to be, is far from fitted yet to the grand tasks of the day. If we try to rise above this chasm and to judge matters from the point of view of a long-term human evolution, we might sum up our observations in the following way:

Man's evolution is the spear-head of the evolution of life, which

A tireless advocate of international cooperation— a theme emphasized in his latest book, "Portrait of Europe"—Professor de Madariaga has written extensively on world affairs. He recently helped found the College of Europe in Belgium. Although a native of Spain, he lives in England.

in turn sets in when physical evolution is well advanced on our planet. Now, the chief point is that the evolution of life brings into the world a principle and a trend in reverse to that of physical evolution. The evolution of matter tends ever towards disintegration, pulverization, equalization. Hills get eaten up by the wind and the rain, seas and rivers get filled up, temperatures get even, and in due course, all ends in a dead, desert-like equality of sand.

Life, however, evolves exactly the opposite way. The amoeba becomes every century more complicated, and gives rise to the lichen, the plant, the animal, man. So, from the amoeba to the Sistine Chapel or the Ninth Symphony, life waxes every day higher, more complex, more independent from direct physical requirements, more unlikely, more unexpected, more original.

This is our challenge to-day. There are those among us who would have us all become equal: all like grains of sand in a desert. That way lies communism. And that way also many misguided forms of strictly equalitarian socialism. These leaders and advisers would drive mankind back to the mineral. They are blind to the true law of man's evolution.

Then there are the nationalists. They would guide us back to the herd. For these people, a nation is like a herd of elephants, of buffaloes or of giraffes; and they remain incapable of rising above the interests and power of their own kith and kin. These people are not as reactionary as the communists, for they would not drive mankind back as far as the grain of sand; but they certainly would drive it backwards, towards the animal.

The challenge of our day demands that we should give up the dream of deadly equality and the nightmare of murderous nationalism: in order to rise to the conception of a well organized mankind, conscious of its common spirit, and constituted in tiers of federations of free communities capable of cooperating in peace and liberty.

As a token of sound policy showing that the leading nations are on the right path, I should like to see the internationalization of mineral oil, uranium and civil aviation, limited at first, of course, to the non-communist world.

The Fabulous Future

DAVID SARNOFF

The dominant physical fact in the next quarter-century will be technological progress unprecedented in kind and in volume. In relation to the total history of the human race, the last hundred years have been no more than a split second. Yet they have compassed more technological achievement than the millennia that preceded. The harnessing of electricity to the purposes of light, power and communication; the demonstration of the germ theory of disease; discovery and application of the electron; invention of radio and television; development of anesthetics; the exploration of genes and mutations; invention of motor vehicles; evolution of the assembly line and other mass-production techniques; proliferation of organic chemistry; the splitting of the atom; development of antibiotics; the vast expansion of the known and measured universe of stars and galaxies—these are only the highlights of recent progress.

And it is not just a case of continued increase but of continued acceleration of increase. We need only project the curve into the future to realize that we are merely on the threshold of the technological age.

There is no longer margin for doubt that whatever the mind of man visualizes, the genius of modern science can turn into fact. The released energies of the atom, though born in war and baptized in destruction, are already being funneled to man's constructive purposes.

Other sources of energy—the sun, the tides, and the winds—are certain to be developed beyond present expectations. New

Pioneer in the American communications industry, General Sarnoff has contributed much to the development of electronics radio and television in the United States. As chairman of the board of the Radio Corporation of America, he directs one of the world's largest communications enterprises.

50

materials by the score — metals, fabrics, woods, glass — will be added to the hundreds of synthetics already available. Fresh water purified from the briny seas will enable us to make deserts flourish and to open to human habitation immense surfaces of the globe now sterile or inaccessible. Tidelands and the ocean floors beyond, already being tapped for oil, will be increasingly mined for other materials and harvested for chemical and food resources.

Medicine can look to incalculable aid from science and technology. Similarly, techniques for learning faster and better will be opened up by color television, improved means of communication, electronic magnification, and other new processes.

We have a right to make the same kind of projection for social progress, though with far less assurance. The material triumphs now at our disposal must be translated into a happier life for mankind everywhere.

High among our goals must be greater mutual tolerance among races and nationalities. We cannot wholly weed out the primeval prejudices and fears in the jungle undergrowth of the human mind. But we can remove some and neutralize the effects of the rest.

The reduction of crime—by individuals and by nations—also deserves a priority in our hopes and plans. The ever more plentiful supplies of food and goods, higher standards of living and education and health—these should make the containment of violence easier during the coming years.

Automation and other aspects of scientific advance will, as a matter of course, put a premium on brains rather than brawn. One hopes that in the years ahead a decent education will have become as indispensable as a decent suit of clothes. Not labor but leisure will be the great problem in the decades ahead. That prospect should be accepted as a God-given opportunity to add dimensions of enjoyment and grace to life. We have reason to foresee a fantastic rise in demand for and appreciation of the better, and perhaps the best, in art, music and letters.

In small things and large, in greater conveniences and a greater recognition of our common humanity, the quarter-century awaits us in a mood of welcome. We must resolve to fulfill its thrilling promises. Should we fail, the fault will not be with science and technology but with ourselves.

Now, perhaps the most futile intellectual exercise is the discussion as to whether an industrialized society is "desirable." We might as reasonably argue whether the tides and the seasons are desirable. The genie of science could not be stuffed back into the bottle even if we so wished.

But aside from the academic nature of the question, the claim that there is an inherent conflict between science and our immortal souls does not stand up under examination. True, the marvels of technology have come upon us so suddenly that they have created problems of adjustment. But on the whole the adjustment has been remarkably good. America, the classic land of technology, enjoys the largest freedom from destitution, ignorance and disease, along with political rights and social improvements unique in history.

It seems to me unqualifiedly good that more and more of the weight of arduous toil will be unloaded onto the backs of machines; that the sum total of pain and agony will be further reduced by the progress of healing; that modern communications will bring peoples and nations into closer contact, leading to better understanding of one another.

The coming decades will, however, be marked by great challenges to our courage, character, wisdom and stamina. The greatest of these challenges, of course, will be the continuing Communist drive for world dominion.

If freedom is lost, if the dignity of man is destroyed, advances on the material plan will not be "progress" but a foundation for a new savagery. Mankind cannot indefinitely carry the mounting burdens of an armaments race, and the greater burdens of fear and uncertainty.

Our supreme commitment, as we look to the crucial decades ahead, must be to win the peace — not a peace of totalitarian dominion but a genuine peace rooted in liberty. I believe it can be done.

The Mind of Man Reaches Out

CARL GUSTAV JUNG

Without doubt we are on the eve of a new age which will pose some difficult questions. To forecast future developments in psychology and in our knowledge of mental disease and treatment, is no easy task. I prefer to refrain from incompetent attempts at prophecy and to present my opinion as the hopes of a doctor and student of mental illness living in the beginning of the second half of the twentieth century.

The most common mental disease — the one which therefore poses the greatest problem to the various societies of the world— is schizophrenia. (Schizophrenia is a form of mental disease in which the patient loses touch with the real world and may develop fantastic delusions). The psychology of schizophrenia is still in a rather unsatisfactory state. Not much progress has been made in this still unexplored region since my own studies were published fifty years ago.

Although I have observed, analyzed and treated a fair number of schizophrenics in the interval, I could not carry through a systematic study. Let us look more closely at this disease and its symptoms, and see why it has defied systematic study.

Schizophrenic symptoms rather resemble what takes place in dreams or states of intoxication. That is, there is a lowering of the mental level—an inability to concentrate or pay attention. The patient misses the connection between the words in a sentence. Finally, not only the meaning of the phrase but also the words themselves are lost. Moreover, strange, disconnected and illogical intrusions on the mind make impossible any continuity of thought. Now many people—because of emotional disturbances

---

A founder of modern psychiatry, Dr. Jung is one of the world's great experts on the human mind. He has made trail-blazing contributions to our understanding of mental illness. Although over eighty years old, he is still active as practising therapist and scientific scholar.

of one kind or another—may find themselves less able than for-
merly to pay attention or to concentrate. They may daydream, for
instance. But their illusions are coherent. The schizophrenic
complex, on the other hand, is characterized by a peculiar disintegration of its own representations. The content of the illusion
is fragmentized by the fact that the patient—the man having the
illusion—has lost the ability for coordinated thinking and speech.

Now the reason there has been so little progress made in the
treatment or understanding of schizophrenia is that scientists cannot study disease of itself. They must study disease as it relates
to health, as it departs from health, as it differs from health. This
is what we lack in the study of schizophrenia. For no known psychological processes—in either normal or neurotic people—parallel in any degree whatsoever the way the schizophrenic fragmen-
tizes the content of his illusion.

We get no clue to schizophrenia, therefore, from more healthy
processes. However, one may conceive of the peculiar behavior
of the schizophrenic complex, its difference from that of the neurotic or normal complex is obvious. Moreover, inasmuch as we
have been unable to discover any psychologically understandable
process to account for the schizophrenic complex, I draw the conclusion that there might be a toxic cause. The toxic cause may
in turn be due to an organic and local breakdown. That is to say,
a physiological change has taken place because the brain cells
were subjected to emotional stress beyond their capacity. Experience with a drug called mescaline, and related drugs, definitely
encourages the theory that schizophrenic symptoms are toxic in
origin.

Looking toward future developments in the field of psychiatry,
I suggest that here is an almost unexplored region, ready for
pioneering research work.

The search for the specific toxin is a task for clinical psychiatry.
For the psychopathologist and for the psychologist of the future,
the task ahead is to study the delusions of schizophrenia and their
meaning. It is a known fact, which I proved to my own satisfac-
tion fifty years ago, that the disease can be treated—although to a

limited extent—by psychotherapy. But as soon as one tries psychological treatment, the question comes up of the psychotic contents of schizophrenia, and their meaning.

Now, as I've said, the contents of a neurosis can be explained
by the data of personal biography. But psychotic contents—schzi-
phrenic delusions—cannot. They defy any purely personalistic
interpretation.

Indeed, the contents of the psychotic delusion suggests something which the patient did not personally acquire—but which is
rather a part of the *collective nature of the human mind*. These
delusions show an analogy not to ordinary dreams—but to the type
of dreams which primitive people call "big dreams." The imagery
of "big dreams" is related to mythology. Such images occur in
the lore of primitive tribes, in ancient myths—as well as in the
dreams, visions and delusions of modern indivduals who are entirely ignorant of those traditions.

I am suggesting that beyond the personally acquired contents
of the personal subconscious mind of each of us, there is a
deeper stratum—a stratum of the collective unconscious mind of
the human race. And any research into such realms cannot be
dealt with on the basis of merely individual psychology. Such
research leads inevitably to the problem of the human mind *in
toto*. And research in this field is in its infancy. There is a
magnificent opportunity ahead for increasing our understanding
of the human mind.

The Immediate Biological Future

HERMANN J. MULLER

The five years already elapsed since the mid-point of the twentieth century have brought startling advances in our knowledge of the nature of living matter and also in our techniques of investigating it. Judging by these advances we may achieve far greater victories in this field before the end of our own century than had seemed possible five years ago.

There have been several remarkable break-throughs in this field recently. Among these perhaps the foremost are the findings made by Watson, Crick, Hershey, Stanley and others, in the exploration of the material that forms the basis of heredity, the genes. The findings show that these genes are molecules which have the form of long chains. In any given chain, or gene, there are thousands of links, which are called nucleotides, but these links are of only four standard types. The exact arrangement of these four kinds of links in line in any gene decides how that gene will reach emically and therefore what biological functions it will serve. Each chain has the ability to gather to itself scattered links or nucleotides from out of the surrounding fluid and to arrange them into a pattern just like its own. In this way it reproduces itself. The chemical principles by which this reproduction happens are even now being worked out.

These findings already afford unexpected insight into the most fundamental attributes of living things—how like begets like and how things grow. More is also becoming known about the exceptions to the rule of like begetting like, that is, the sudden changes in genes called mutations. It is these mutations which furnish the

---

Winner of a Nobel Prize for his discoveries in the field of genetics, Dr. Muller is credited with being the discoverer of the technique of producing mutations by means of X-ray. He has been a member of the faculty of Indiana University since 1945. He is the President of the Society for the Study of Evolution and of the American Humanist Association.

"building blocks" of evolution. The new findings show that mutations consist of alterations in the pattern of the nucleotides, involving substitutions or rearrangements of them. Some of the best informed students of this subject believe that it may even be possible, rather soon, to pick these chains to bits, piece by piece, so as to discover the details of the arrangements. If this can be done perhaps we will also be able to reconstruct the chains, and even to synthesize new chain patterns more or less at will. In some simpler organisms such synthetic chains might then be implanted within them.

All these accomplishments would not yet allow us to create the mutations we want to and so to endow living things with chosen, desired characteristics. Before this could be done we should also have to find out how the genes function in producing the other materials of living things. More especially we would need to know how the genes produced the materials called proteins, since these proteins form the bulk of living things and carry out their more conspicuous activities. However, there are indications in the work of Paulnig, Lipmann, Gamow, Spiegelman, Beadle, du Vigneaud, and many others, of break-throughs occurring on this front also. These should furnish information concerning the method by which the genes produce the proteins, concerning the detailed composition of these proteins, and the ways in which they in their turn influence the course of the diverse chemical operations of living things. The provision by the nuclear physicists of atoms identifiable by their radioactivity is one factor of major importance in the further prosecution of such investigations.

These findings concerning the basic materials of life will provide means for a more effective attack upon the problem of the origin of life. Other means will be provided by the newer geology, utilizing the contributions of astrophysics and physical chemistry, as exemplified in the work of Urey, Kuiper and others. In addition, there will be direct experimental investigation of the manner in which they would naturally combine to produce the simplest things. It seems not at all impossible also that, before the century's end, space flight will have succeeded to the point of bringing back samples of the living things of Mars. A study of these specimens will undoubtedly present some striking chemical contrasts with terrestrial organisms, as well as some striking similarities. We will thereby greatly advance our knowledge concerning the origin of life and concerning the most basic possibilities of living things.

Another biological field in which significant progress is likely in the coming decades is that of the nature of the processes of development and differentiation from the egg through the embryonic periods and those of youth, adulthood and old age, as well as in regeneration. Techniques different from those most commonly used on these problems in the past are, however, needed for breakthroughs here. It may be that these will be provided in part by combining the methods of immunology, as in Soneborn's work; of transference of nuclei and other cell constituents, as in Briggs' work; and of the culturing of individual cells of higher organisms, as in the work of Puck. Such information should tell us a great deal about how living things develop normally and also about how they develop in abnormal cases, as for instance in cancer. And with such knowledge we should gain increasing means of controlling these events.

Of all the operations of higher organisms the greatest challenge is provided by those of the central nervous system, especially the brain. There are indications that important light will be thrown on the age-old problem of the relation of consciousness to the workings of the brain in the next half century by a number of methods of attack. One of these methods involves delicate study, by both electrical and biochemical means, of individual nerve cells and of relatively simple groups of interconnected nerve cells. Another method involves observations of the effects of directly stimulating and otherwise treating given cells and cell-groups as they lie within the central nervous system. It seems probable that some of these experimenters will perform their observations on themselves, thus gaining simultaneous inner and outer views of the same phenomena.

However great our progress in understanding and influencing

the development and the functioning of the body, there will always be limits to its control by these means. These limits are set by the potentialities of its genes. Now, the mutations of these genes cause these limits to be changed, but the changes are usually for the worse. This is a subject for concern. For although the less fit individuals, resulting from the undesirable changes, tend to die out in a state of nature, this is not necessarily true today. It has therefore become important to increase our scanty knowledge of mutation in man. This means that we must find out much more about the frequency of mutations, about what agents promote or hinder their occurrence, about the numbers of mutations having different kinds of effects, and about how the individuals with mutated genes spread or decline in numbers in the population in successive generations. All this knowledge is especially necessary in the atomic age because radiation is a potent agent in producing mutations. The obtaining of such information will require very large-scale genetic investigations on such types as microbes, fruit flies, and mice. In addition there must be much more extensive and more refined observations of inheritance in man and experiments like those of Puck, on the production of mutations in human cells cultured outside of the body, after the fashion of microbes. Undoubtedly great advances will be made at the same time in the means of controlling reproduction. These advances should make it the more possible for all this knowledge ultimately to be of service in the genetic betterment of humanity.

Economic Trends and Problems

Most countries throughout the world have for the last ten years been living through a period of rapid economic growth. This is a great change from the state of affairs in the 1930's, a period of depression and unemployment, for which those who exercised authority at that time must accept responsibility. It was the chronic depression of the 1930's which gave some justification to those people, in different countries, who began to believe that the world's era of economic growth was over, and that economic stagnation would be the rule of the future.

Although considerable poverty and unemployment still exist, public opinion in most countries has now come to take economic growth for granted. Indeed the ordinary citizen is entitled to expect that those who control the economic policy of his country, with all the wealth and technical resources which they have at their disposal, will be able to maintain economic growth, and he is fully justified in criticising them if they do not.

The rate at which productivity can be improved is, however, limited. If we measure productivity by the quantity of goods and services produced, per man hour of labor performed, we find, for instance, in the U.S.A. that this has been growing ever since the 19th century at a steady rate of about two and one quarter per cent per year. Most other industrial countries show similar figures. It is rare for the figure for rate of growth to go as high as three per cent per year, and figures above that only occur under exceptional circumstances. In Soviet Russia productivity is growing but at a lesser rate than in many of the western industrial countries. Japan has now had a high economic growth rate for more

---

An eminent Australian economist, Colin Clark is a member of the faculty of Oxford University in England. Since 1953 he has been director of Oxford's Institute for Research in Agricultural Economics.

than half a century.   India, after a long period of comparative stagnation, is now also developing a high growth rate.   Prospects of economic growth are as inviting for Asian countries as for European.

It was, however, a leading American statistician, Professor Kuznetz, who pointed out that the world's economic growth had been very uneven.   In the middle of the 19th century, the world was much poorer than it is now, but the discrepancies between the poor and the wealthy countries were probably less then than they are now.

These discrepancies will eventually be removed, but inevitably they will persist for a long time.   The process of poorer communities catching up with richer is one of which we can watch an example, for instance, in the southern states of the U. S. where the rate of growth of real income per head is now much higher than in the northern states, and the economic differences between are therefore quickly disappearing.

It remains, however, to state the elementary but sometimes forgotten truth that it is only through increasing productivity that the world in general, and the poorer nations in particular, can be enriched.   People sometimes speak of one country enriching itself at the expense of others.   While a number of such cases of economic injustice have occurred, the amount of wealth obtained by one country from exploitation or investments in another, or from any particular advantages which it has obtained for itself in the way of supply of raw materials, of markets or of capital, is always found on examination to be trivial compared with the wealth obtained from its own productivity.   The complete removal from the world of all such injustices between countries as still remain would now make very little difference to the comparative wealth of countries, and great increases in productivity would still be called for.

One of the principal obstacles to the growth of productivity has been the false concept of economics disseminated by Marxians, who teach that, unless all means of production are transferred to public ownership, labor cannot secure any advantage from

increasing productivity, and that labor's share in the product must
always be falling. This theory is so flatly contradicted by all the
facts that those who propagate it must either be very ignorant
men, or unfortunately, in a few cases, well-informed men who are
deliberately setting out to pervert the truth. In the industrial
countries of North America and Western Europe the share of
labor in the national product has been increasing, and labor receives between seventy and eighty per cent of the whole net national product.

Some people, however, may still be impatient at the comparatively slow rate at which productivity can advance, even in the
developed countries. They may ask whether we should not expect a great acceleration in the future, in view of the use of automatically controlled machinery, and of the greater rate of scientific and technical discovery.

What really matters for this purpose, however, is not the rate
at which scientific and technical discoveries are made, but the rate
at which men can use them. This, in turn, depends upon the rate
at which we can build up the necessary economic organization, and
train men to perform new tasks. There are limits to the rate at
which we can do these things, dependent upon our human material, however fast the scientists and technicians provide us with
new knowledge. Education will probably prove to be, in the
long run, the most important of all factors in economic progress.

To sum up, therefore, I think that some increase in the rate of
economic growth may be possible in a number of countries, but
that it cannot be spectacular; and that the poorer countries, one
by one, will do what India is doing now, and increase their productivity at a pace which will eventually enable them to catch up
with the wealthier countries. But that process will take a long
time.

The Coming Generation of Scientists

GUNNAR RANDERS

Twenty years ago people would have stared blankly at anyone presenting himself as a nuclear engineer. Today there are 5,000 of these specialists in the United States alone. In twenty years, it is expected that there will be a need for 50,000, or ten times as many.

In those next twenty years—up until 1975—it is by no means expected that the total population will increase tenfold.

Does it mean that we are moving towards a period in which the whole population will become nuclear engineers? No, it does not. One reason for the extremely rapid increase is that nuclear energy is still a young and fast-growing development. However, new, fast-growing technical developments seem to be springing up more and more frequently, and even if one considers the total number of scientists and engineers, not only nuclear specialists, it appears that their number is growing very much faster relatively than the total population. So, indications at least are that we are moving toward a future world with a highly scientific and technically-inclined population.

Many people deplore such a development. "How sad to have a world full of scientific, technical specialists!", they say, or: "To bad that we happen to live in an unfortunate period when the hap-hazard fluctuations of evolution produce a golden age for egg-heads and bookworms."

It is not as simple as that. The growing demand for scientific and technical education is more than an accidental fluctuation.

Norway's most distinguished nuclear physicist, Dr. Randers began his career as an astrayphysicst but later turned toward atomic research. He helped set up the joint Norwegian-Dutch atomic reactor laboratory and was the driving spirit behind the European Atomic Energy Society. Since 1954 he has been special advisor on atomic energy to the Secretary-General of the United Nations.

It is really the symptom of the deepest change, of the most fundamental development in human society—a development which has been going on for hundreds of years and which will continue. It shows the steady evolution from superstition and ignorance towards rational thinking and knowledge. It indicates the spreading of the scientific method from the old, narrow limits of physics and chemistry to the daily life of people. The increasing application of technical means in one's life is only *one* of the aspects of the gradual growth of the ability to think and act rationally, to master the mysteries of nature instead of being scared of them.

Today, the method of inquiring into unknown problems, without preconceived opinions, without prejudices, — the method of building up knowledge painstakingly by adding to the solid foundations of proven knowledge—begins to take over from the ancient method of trying, by the powers of witchcraft and sorcery, to obtain one's goals. It is not so much the new technical facilities which create the trend toward a scientifically-inclined population. It is the acceptance of honest, methodical inquiry in all problems —from child psychology to advertising methods—which is changing our society and making scientific training as essential in the future as good manners were in the old days.

So, there is no way back. There is no hope that the present clamoring for great numbers of new scientists and engineers shall, by another fluctuation, be replaced by a clamoring for great numbers of poets and painters—however desirable many would find such a thought.

It is civilization itself which requires human society to have more people with a greater knowledge of nature and of the manner in which nature works.

We must remember that this development has been going on a long time. Any high school graduate today would have ranked as a highly-qualified natural scientist in most communities three hundred years ago. And all indications are that the general scientifiic understanding of today's average engineer will be commonplace among high school graduates in a hundred years or so.

Perhaps some will ask what all the scientists will do in the future. Are not the basic principles of our modern science practically worked out? With atomic power a technical reality and even thermo-nuclear energy release achieved—although as yet in an uncontrolled way—have we not reached close to the final limit?

It would be a great mistake to believe that we have nearly reached the limit of scientific knowledge. Fifty years ago it was not even possible to know that anything existed inside the atomic nucleus which would be worth studying. As a matter of fact, it was not even known that the nucleus existed. Today we cannot guess what problems scientists will face in 50 years.

The field of biology, the study of life itself, has hardly begun. Only the last decades have seen basic progress begin to appear in this field.

In spite of our apparent mastery of the atom, we do not yet have a satisfactory theory or understanding of the elementary particles with which we are working.

Serious experimental scientific research has only existed in the world a few hundred years—and all indications are that we have still some billions of years to go on the earth. So, it is too early to give up and believe we are near the end of scientific development—or what is the same, near the end of discovering the true relationships of the multitude of phenomena confronting us in our daily lives on this planet. We have hardly peeked in through the keyhole.

But one thing we have discovered during the last decade: If scientists had not worked up the long road of research and development to atomic energy, there would today have been no hope of ever providing the energy required to lift the world's population to the level of material standards of the Western world. The only thinkable future would have been a lowering of Western standards to provide reasonable material equality in the world—a necessary requirement for lasting peace.

The lesson is, therefore, to appreciate the value of free scientific inquiry and to realize that it forms the basis for the future of civilization.

The development we are discussing is by no means deplorable

or dull. Nature itself is more fantastic than the tricks of any accomplished sorcerer. Nature has more power than any imagined witchcraft.

Life in a modern, technical civilization, as we experience it every day, is free from so many of the sufferings and privations of former times that we have nearly forgotten them.

And only the growth of science and technique, in effect the very efforts of our coming generation of nuclear engineers and scientists, can give hope for a future world where *all* human beings can enjoy the advanced civilization after which we all are striving.

New Ways of Living

WILLIAM ZECKENDORF

How will the changes brought about by new sources of power, by new scientific and medical discoveries, by increased industrialization—how will all these changes affect the way in which people actually live? By "actually" I mean the way in which they live together—in cities. For it is about city living that I feel qualified to talk.

The lives of millions upon millions of people wil be more or less rewarding during the next half century, according to how well and how intelligently the city of the future is planned. This is true not only in the nations which are now highly industrialized but in those in which industrialization lies ahead.

I should say that the unsatisfactory cities we have known in the past have not been the exclusive product of either the industrial or the non-industrial society. They have been the result of lack of planning. The chaotic result—the disordered, unplanned, congested, slum-ridden city—has happened in a shorter space of time, it is true, in societies which have become rapidly industrialized. But they have grown up just as surely—indeed more disease-ridden, more poverty-ridden—in societies far removed from the advance of industry.

The problem ahead, then, is a universal one. One aspect of it is to wipe out the slum areas and the areas of sickness within our cities. This can be done in a matter of years.

The other aspect of the problem is to make our cities over so that they are more livable. And here, indeed, is the challenge. It will require greater imagination, greater resources, greater patience.

I shall not attempt here to describe the Utopian city, but I think

One of America's most imaginative planners and builders, Mr. Zeckendorf is president of a large New York real estate firm. He has combined theory about urban living with the practical knowledge that comes from actually developing or redeveloping massive urban areas.

a word should be said about what we want to achieve. We are going to build cities which are complete settings for office and commercial buildings, for residential and cultural units, for people of every age and income. Therefore our thinking must be all-inclusive. We must have the view of the real estate economist, the planner, the architect, the traffic expert, and those who can see that the city offers recreational opportunities for all its people. Architecture must give modern dimension and expression to the dignity of man within a society becoming industrialized.

Now—as to how to achieve this. I think that in a democratic society, the most intelligent and imaginative planning will come from a combination of public and private agencies working together.

The public agency—that is the city—must have the right to zone. It must be able to say: "Let us place our highest office buildings here, our smaller ones there. Let us put our light and semi-heavy and heavy industries in this area, where they logically go with utilities and transportation centers. Since we are going to have theaters," the city must be able to say, "let them have a logical relationship to the things connected with them—the hotels, dining places and perhaps opera, music, ballet and allied arts." The city must protect its zoning plan by preventing irrational and haphazard building. Residences should be kept to appropriate areas, and industrial activity should not encroach on residential areas or office space areas. In order to protect the community, such limitations must be set.

But within the framework of the general community plan, indi-demic. The private builder, again within the framework of the viduals must be free to exercise their ingenuity. Individuals, developing the plan in detail. And private enterprise should not be looked upon by public agencies as the vehicle for carrying out private businessmen and builders should have the responsibility of official doctrines. Planning by a public agency tends to be aca-stages the areas for which he will be ultimately responsible. The community plan, should have the right to plan at the earliest

result is likely to be a revitalized city and an imaginative development of which both city and individual can be proud.

The relationship between city authorities and private businessmen in meeting the challenge of the city of the future should be
one of mutual open-mindedness. Pride of authorship should be
forgotten in the interests of all, and the planning authorities should
encourage the submission of plans by creative private individuals.
This will assure that all men in the community are making their
best contribution toward a living environment.

The future is bound to bring more, not less, city-dwelling. We
have nothing to fear from such a prospect. Cities can be things
of beauty and light. Let us see that they are.

The Progress of Medical Science

FRANK MACFARLANE BURNET

I believe that the primary objective of medical science can be broadly stated as "to provide for every human being the greatest measure of health and length of life that is allowed by his bodily inheritance."

Implicit in that statement is the realization that has grown up in the last fifty years of the significance of genetic factors in human medicine. If there is any central theme in this brief talk, it is that the hope of healthy, happy and long-lived generations to follow us will not be fulfilled unless we can widen the scope of preventive medicine to include care for the well-being of the human species as a whole, as well as of the individuals who compose it.

My own interest in medicine has been centered on the prevention and treatment of infectious disease. It has been a **very** great privilege to watch at relatively close quarters the closing stages of that conquest of infectious disease which future historians may class as the most important social revolution of the past eighty years. Today there are prove dand practical ways by which all the great pestilences of history can be prevented. Even in the midst of war, plague, cholera and typhus, yellow fever, smallpox and malaria, can all be rendered harmless. It is probably not unduly optimistic to say that given energy and goodwill, the application of available knowledge could render every country in the world as free of infectious disease as Scandinavia and New Zealand are today.

There is of course another side to the picture. Everyone who

A renowned microbiologist, Sir Macfarlane has won world recognition for his contributions to the control of infectious diseases. As a microbiologist and virologist, he has developed techniques which have helped isolate the viruses of several diseases—including those of influenza and poliomyelitis. Since 1944 he has been the director of the Walter and Eliza Hall Institute of Medical Research in Melbourne, Australia.

has watched the changes in human population that have taken place over the last fifty years knows that the control of infectious disease is almost solely responsible for the present great surge of population in the less advanced countries of the world. Until the 19th century, the toll of childhood deaths from infectious disease was so high that a birth rate of something over forty per one thousand per annum was necessary to allow a slow growth of population. If, while such a birth rate persists, modern health measures bring the death rate down to ten or twelve per thousand, it is a very simple sum to show that for a time at least the population will double every thirty years. That is what is happening in Ceylon at the present time. It is beyond argument that success in controlling infectious disease and other causes of premature death will eventually demand an equivalent success in controlling the birth rate. Despite all the difficulties in the way, it is a major task of medical science to find practical and socially acceptable means by which this can be achieved. Health in the future will only be possible if over-population with its attendant evils, can be avoided.

Provided we can look forward to a level of world population commensurate with natural resources, present knowledge should ensure that malnutrition and infectious disease will become almost negligible as causes of death. This will mean a sharp break with the past, but it will not mean that all our medical problems will be solved.

Now and in the future, the tasks of preventive medicine will lie in two main directions. First, to recognize and prevent disease arising from changes in our ways of life and in our physical environment. Second, to elucidate the part played by inheritance in human disease and disability; and to design action, in the first instance, to remedy or alleviate such disability. Eventually, it may become possible and necessary to take positive steps to improve the inheritance of future generations.

I can only touch on these very briefly. At the present time there are two important diseases which in highly developed countries are showing a steady increase in mortality—cancer of the lung and leukemia. There is still controversy over the meaning of these increases, but it is highly significant—first, that excessive cigarette smoking is associated with a large increase in the incidence of lung cancer; and second, that exposure to penetrating radiation — X-rays, atomic explosions, radioactive materials — is a potent cause of leukemia. Such effects of changing circumstances are from their nature preventible—and those concerned with health in industry have had long experience in dealing with comparable problems on a smaller scale. But constant vigilance will obviously be needed.

I have stressed the significance of the genetic approach. We probably tend to forget how, at the present time, a very large proportion of medical care is directed toward overcoming major or minor genetic weakness. Such things as spectacles, hearing aids and artificial dentures are completely unexciting and mildly embarrassing to mention, but they have probably done more for human comfort and happiness than anything else in medicine. In the future there will be increasing technical improvement in these things, and we shall probably see increasingly bold and effective use of surgery to remedy major genetic defects.

Most mental abnormality has a genetic basis—and the future will undoubtedly see an intensified search for ways in which, despite his inherited weakness, the individual can find a satisfying place in the community. In the last year or two we have seen the very heartening and unexpected discovery that the new drugs of reserpine and chlorpromazine can do much to bring a large group of sufferers back to social usefulness. This has already initiated a new wave of interest in the effect of chemical substances on mental processes, and further advances in treatment may be expected in the future.

With better understanding of the nature and extent of genetic weaknesses, there will undoubtedly be an increasing interest in what is nowadays called the eugenic approach. Racial deterioration is difficult to define and will always be a slow process, invisible to a single generation. But unless all the teaching of genetics and evolution is inapplicable to man, genetic deterioration is in the long run inevitable, unless medical science can find a good substitute to replace the bitter struggle for existence that prevented such deterioration in the past.

That, I believe, is the last and the greatest objective of medicine for the future.

Propaganda and New Ideas

WALT DISNEY

To attempt to predict the nature and the course of mass communication during the next half century is a questionable thing, even on the basis of what has been achieved during the past fifty years. That it must mark a new era in the commingling of ideas and intelligence toward the shaping of a better global civilization we may, however, cheerfully anticipate.

Mechanisms so rapidly developed within the past few decades— radio, television, motion pictures, recordings—which may address millions of people in the same hour across the earth—have provided the means. And yet many of these millions are still strangers to other millions. Much of the best and most promising in the life of whole regions has thus far been jealously guarded and excluded from these fraternal overtures.

So, it is to the *nature* of our communications that we must look for the benefactions which can come from such interchange. The machinery stands ready, is already widely in use and will become perhaps incredibly more so as we put science to our humanitarian uses.

What we say to one another, across continents and oceans, as well as within our own immediate national boundaries—this will tell how ready we are to achieve closer bonds in the great family of man. Honesty will be the code word—the keynote. Only complete candor will ever achieve what is ideally desirable in this respect. Only complete honesty will do justice to any people who

---

Innovator extraordinary in the realm of mass communication, Mr. Disney is one of Hollywood's most ingenious motion picture producers. Since launching his first animated cartoons in 1928, with Mickey Mouse as his star, Mr. Disney's characters have competed with those of the most cherished fairytales. In 1935 he received the French Legion of Honor Award for "creating a new art form spreading good will throughout the world."

seek the essential friendship of other folk. And unless mass communication of ideas and ideals in the broad sense is so founded, it will be a sham and have an ulterior intent.

At present, as I view it, there is still much of what we have come to call propaganda in the prepared and restricted international exchange of knowledge and social ideas. Every nation practices it. It is of course a natural impulse to put the best foot forward. It is a defensive gesture, as if we were to say we are fearful of the whole truth about ourselves.

But, I think we are entitled to believe that we are heading toward a period of more amiable world intercourse. I believe it despite sometimes gloomy portents.

I have come to put great reliance on the value of fact and forthrightness in things that concern people most vitally. It has been demonstrated over and over during the past few years in my profession and my observation. Facts about nature and humankind, even when occasionally they are not exactly idyllic, beget confidence. Truth rather than fiction, even when it encounters stubborn prejudices, is reliable. It gives us more predictable guidance in all our relationships.

Furthermore, I believe every people in the multitude of nations owes it to every other tribe of the human family—now so close together on a shrinking planet—to communicate freely in matters of common concern. If it is truly the desire to cement a closer neighborliness and tolerance in this so often strife-torn globe, then there should be no need for curtains of any kind to keep information in or out about any land or folk.

In dealing with assorted humans all over the earth in our profession, I have been deeply impressed with the almost pathetic eagerness of people to know one another better; to believe the best about one another. They want to laugh together at things which touch a common chord—not look askance at folk across some sea or boundary line. They have a bond which says we are all much alike and have a common destiny—if only we can understand one another in our ceaseless struggle toward what we believe to be a finer civilization through our various cultures.

Inventions, discoveries pertaining to use of great vital resources —as lately the promise of peaceable use of atomic energy—have tremendous bearing on civilizations and the ultimate fate of global society. None more so, it seems to me, than those facilities having to do with quicker and wider transmission of information.

It seems reasonable to suppose, as the pace of science now indicates, that almost every hamlet, every family, if not every adult individual across the face of the earth will have portable receivers attuned to all broadcast sources. They may be worn as today a shirt button or a cuff link is worn. Other transmission rays, even, may be employed. And in the face of such universal communication—as if one were to chat to a neighbor across the street—many if not all old belligerent passions, fears, suspicions, contentions may well be allayed to favor better understanding and more sympathetic relations, closer and deeper humanities.

The implements will be ready.

The truth and the whole revealing truth, even though it may at times seem a fault to be disguised or dissembled! That seems to me to be the purpose and the goal of mass communication in the predictable future, whatever the broadcasting machinery may be. To understand another's problems and struggles in the universal human dilemma is a far more effective means toward friendly and compassionate interest than any boasted superiority or perfection.

New Realms of Art

HERBERT READ

Prediction is hazardous in any sphere of human activity, and the arts are perhaps especially wayward. The changes during the first half of this century of ours have been bewildering, and if we go back another half-century we can say that within a hundred years—a short time in the history of civilization—there has occurred a revolution so fundamental that we must search many past centuries for a parallel. Possibly the only comparable change is the one that took place between the Old and the New Stone Age, when an organic animal art was replaced by an abstract geometrical art.

This comparison is not too far-fetched because there was, in those distant prehistoric times, a fundamental change in social habits—a nomadic hunting economy was replaced by a settled productive economy. The new geometric art of the neolithic period was accompanied by practical discoveries like weaving and basket-making; and in a similar way the new art of our own time has been accompanied by a great technological revolution. It would, however, be misleading to suggest that there is causal connection between the two contemporary events. It is true that some of the Impressionists, for example, read scientific treatises on color harmony and tried to incorporate such scientific knowledge in their painting methods. But they were Impressionists first. Behind their interest in science was an overwhelming desire to see the world as if for the first time, in all its natural purity of color, its intensity and movement. If we then try to trace the origins of this desire—we are led back to painters like Delacroix

One of Britain's most provocative and searching art critics and creative writers, Sir Herbert is widely known for his literary appreciations, his essays on modern art, and his philosophical inquiries into the various art forms. His books include novels, collections of poetry, and essays.

and Constable—and from them to that general movement of the spirit known as Romanticism. If we then begin to trace the origins of Romanticism we find ourselves led back to that much more fundamental change in outlook which we call the Renaissance, the humanistic revolution that occurred five or six centuries ago.

It is necessary to look back in this way before we can look forward—because, though the changes in our time have been so revolutionary, they all stem from that decisive moment in European history when man began to look within himself and find there a subject worthy of contemplation. The history of modern art is the gradual discovery of the Self—the expression, in every sensuous medium, of the interior world of the Self, its feelings and sensations, its passions and aspirations, its uniqueness and integrity. This universal tendency, this committal to subjectivity in all its variety and obscurity, explains the bewildering confusion of modern art.

The most recent tendencies in art, and those which we may expect to be prolonged during the next half-century, have been concerned with the deeper levels of the Self—with what psychologists call the unconscious. Again, it is not a case of artists finding inspiration in science—it is rather the other way around, for if we trace the origins of the theory of the unconscious, for example, we are again led back to the Romantic Movement. The modern artist has always been aware of his dreams, and the fact that he is now trying to represent, not the dream world, but the obscurer feelings or formative energies that lie at an even deeper level of the unconscious, must be regarded as an inevitable development of the subjective trends that began centuries ago.

I cannot say where this development will lead in the next fifty years—but the human mind is one of those frontiers of knowledge under discussion in this symposium, and I believe that the artists of the future will have much to contribute in the way of discovery in this field. At the same time we must all be conscious of the fact that this subjective trend in the arts does not embrace all that in the past we have meant by art. Art, in any complete meaning of the word, is a total aspect of a civilization; it is not to be confined to the personal arts of painting or sculpture. There are public arts, which include architecture and town-planning, the industrial arts, and indeed the visual aspect of every human artefact. There is no place for subjectivity in such arts; here all is governed by absolute qualities of harmony and function. But again a revolution is in progress, and a decisive one.

The revolution consists primarily in the fact that the subjective and objective aspects of art have been separated, to the benefit of both aspects. During the eighteenth and nineteenth centuries there was a confusion, fostered by academies of art and artificial fashions, between the fine arts and the functional arts, with the result that we had no coherent style in either. The reason why the architectural monuments of the 19th century are so monstrous is simply that subjective feelings—in the form of an eclectic taste—were applied to the solution of objective problems. The functional revolution in architecture—carried through by great pioneers like Gropius, Le Corbusier, Mies van der Rohe and Frank Lloyd Wright—is best understood as a rejection of such personalism in architecture. This does not mean a rejection of all human elements—on the contrary, the sense of proportion and harmony upon which the successful solution of a functional problem depends, is a human sense. It is more than that—it is a human possession, for our bodies illustrate it. We can take from the measurements of the human body, as Le Corbusier has done, a scale of ideal proportions with which we can humanize space itself. Greek temples and Gothic cathedrals owe their beauty to the use of such a scale, and the way is now open for the architecture of the future to use a similar scale — one perhaps more human and even more beautiful.

What is true for architecture is true for all the practical arts: they all depend upon the progressive realization of this sense of harmony, this sense that integrates mankind and the universe, and upon which, more than upon any other single factor, depends the structure of an enduring civilization.

Our Changing Economies

SUMNER SLICHTER

The economies of the world are entering a new phase—a phase which sharply differentiates them from the economies of the past. The new phase is a result of the development of science and the application of scientific methods to industry.

At long last mankind has developed such a large body of scientific and technical knowledge and such a variety of apparatus and technical skills that the search for many forms of applied knowledge can be brought within the range of the economic calculus. By that I mean that the chance of discovering the answer to a problem and the cost of making the discovery can be estimated with sufficient accuracy so that a well-informed decision can be made by an enterprise or even by a country concerning the proportion of its resources that can advantageously be devoted to research.

The extension of the economic calculus to the acquisition of scientific and technical knowledge is a revolutionary change far more important than any great specific inventions. It means that for the first time in human history men are able to determine, in a rough way at least, the optimum rate at which the productivity of industry might be improved, and to take steps to bring the actual rate of improvement up to the optimum rate. Even in the countries where technology is most advanced, it is plain that the optimum rate is far above the present rate. Furthermore, it is plain that the rate of discovery that is best for the community is higher than the rate that yields the greatest gain to private enterprises. Hence, there is need to subsidize research in the interest of the community as a whole. Moreover, achievement of the

Professor of Economics at Harvard University, Mr. Slichter is a consultant on economic practice whose advice is widely sought by both business and government. He has written extensively on economic subjects.

best rate of gain in productivity will require great changes in the labor force of all countries—particularly enormous increases in the number of scientists, engineers, and skilled workers.

The great question raised by man's recently achieved power to increase the productivity of industry is: "How will this new power be used?" There are four principal alternatives: First, to make possible an enormous increase in population with little change in the levels of per capita consumption; second, an enormous expansion of armaments, greatly increasing men's ability to destroy one another; third, a great growth in the output of physical civilian goods, putting the necessities of life and most conveniences and semi-luxuries within the reach of everyone; and fourth, a great increase in education and leisure, opening up for the first time in history the cultural achievements of mankind to all persons, not merely to the favored few.

That the last two alternatives are the desirable ones there can be no doubt. Few people realize how far the output of the world falls short of meeting even modest needs. To bring consumption per capita up to the average in the United States would require on the average about a six-fold increase in the world's output—considerably less in some places, much more in other places. But the level of per capita output and consumption in the United States needs to be substantially increased, because at least one-third of the population receives quite small incomes. So great is the need for more goods in some parts of the world that even modern technology cannot provide a satisfactory level of consumption unless some countries are willing to bring about a substantial reduction in their population growth.

The promise of the new economies made possible by the extension of the economic calculus to the acquisition of knowledge will not be fully realized if the result is merely an enormous growth in the physical output of goods. Throughout the ages only a tiny fraction of the human race has had an opportunity to acquire much familiarity with the cultural achievements of men. In order to enjoy the riches of the world's cultures, men need primarily two things: education and leisure.

The amount of education men get even in the advanced countries is still quite limited—partly because, for most people, formal education stops when they go to work. But along with a great growth in education is also needed an enormous increase in men's leisure. Indeed, the spread of leisure is necessary for the spread of education. Certainly, the time is not distant in the advanced industrial countries when men will have far more time available for recreation and leisure than they spend in producing goods. Undoubtedly, the work week should be reduced gradually, both because more output is still urgently needed and because most men are not prepared to make good use of large and sudden additions to their leisure. But the growth in productivity during the next generation will make possible great reductions in the work week.

Thus, the new economies created by bringing research within the economic calculus, and by making advantageous an enormous shift of men and resources to the acquisition of knowledge, will open up the possibility of a great cultural revolution. For the first time in history, hundreds of millions of people will have more or less adequate access to the cultural riches of the world—a reasonable opportunity to read, to travel, to learn languages, to enjoy all aspects of the good life.

The Road of Cooperation

TOYOHIKO KAGAWA

Marxism claims that is teaching, which sanctions violence, is a scientific one. But as long as we depend upon violent change instead of peaceful evolution, we cannot hope for the creation of a peaceful society in the world. What we need today is more organized international cooperation without violence or exploitation.

All civilized countries enjoy the benefits of the Universal Postal Union and the Red Cross organization.

All civilized countries have social security systems to protect people from fear of starvation, sickness, and old age. If we can expand and extend this idea of social security beyond national border lines, I think we can diminish the danger of war to a certain extent. Certainly we should be able to organize internationally in a way which would make wars and exploitation obsolete.

How can we proceed to organize an international social security system? We can attain our objective only through the cooperation of different nations and the awakening of the spirit of all peoples.

The cooperative movement which was started in 1844 at Rochdale near Manchester, England, had four major principles: First, the spirit of non-exploitation; second, respect for human values taking precedence over respect for money or material things; third, industrial democracy; and fouth, educational democracy.

Probably the Rochdale pioneers did not realize they were opening a new road which would ultimately lead to the well-being of all peoples. The Rochdale pioneers' principle transcended all

---

Combining spiritual zeal with practical concern for the welfare of his people, Dr. Kagawa has been a prime mover in Japan's cooperative movement. Besides helping to establish the first labor union in Japan, he has organized farmers, doctors, and fishermen into cooperatives.

religious, racial and political differences—and gave new life to social reform movements.

At the time of Karl Marx, cooperative association in practice had not developed enough to show clearly that it could solve the questions of social and economic evils. Lenin did not understand the fundamental principle of the cooperative association, and therefore he dissolved all cooperative associations throughout the Soviet Union in 1917. Thereafter Russia faced famine—and the lives of nearly 5,000,000 people were lost due to the complete lack of cooperative mechanisms. As a consequence of this bitter experience Lenin belatedly realized the necessity of cooperative associations—and revived the cooperative movement in Russia.

Hitler did not understand the principles of the cooperative association in Germany and tried to dissolve existing associations —but the "Raiffeisen" credit cooperative system in Germany at that time was a combination of the cooperative life insurance with the cooperative credit system, and Hitler was unable to dissolve it.

The "Raiffeisen" credit cooperative system spread to Sweden— and that nation was able to accumulate capital with which to develop foreign trade without the evils of exploitation. Today Sweden exports electric bulbs, manufactured by her cooperative associations, to Norway, Denmark, Finland, and England. If we can develop this system, and profit from foreign trade can be plowed back to the importing countries, we will really have a wonderful world! If exporting countries return to importing countries whatever profit is made in the course of trading, I believe the danger of war will disappear from the earth. I believe we can extend this cooperative system internationally—to protect all peoples from unemployment.

The Universal Postal Union and the International Telegraph Agreement are welcomed by all peoples of the world because they all share benefits equally from them. Similarly, all peoples of the world would receive greater benefits from the world-wide, comprehensive social security system. We should be able to extend the spirit of the "Raiffeisen" cooperative to raise the living standards of underprivileged peoples, and to expand the econo-

mies of under-developed countries. There would be no danger of
war and the well-being of all would be assured. The world-wide,
cooperative social security system wil make it easier for us all
to transcend national and racial discrimination.

We are coming to an age where a victorious war is no longer
possible. Many nations continue to spend fantastic amounts of
money to expand army, navy and air forces — but if total war
breaks out and atomic weapons are used by both sides, *all* human
beings will be annihilated.

Therefore from now on we should use atomic energy for peaceful purposes and develop a universal, comprehensive, cooperative
social security system — including international trade, credit,
health, and educational cooperatives. We should be able to culti-
vate international peace and goodwill, so that there will be no need
to waste money and resources on an armament race.

In sum, what we need today is an evolution of social science—
i.e., the expansion of the cooperative principle to a comprehensive social security system—that can eliminate the causes of war.

Religious Touchstones for Tomorrow

ZAFRULLAH KHAN

The very rapid advance of science and technology during and since the Second World War has ushered in a new era. Mankind stands today at the threshold of a new epoch. The forces now at man's command, which are being daily augmented, hold out the prospect of a vast advance in human welfare and prosperity. They also fill men's minds with fear and dread. The use of weapons which these forces have made possible could destroy culture and civilization and even wipe out human life. The tension between the great powers is a constant reminder of that dread possibility.

Statesmen and men of science are anxiously studying methods for the safeguarding of peace and security against the threat held out by the use of these weapons and of others of even greater power that may be invented. Let us hope and pray that these efforts result in agreements being reached, and preventives becoming available, which may prove adequate. It must be confessed, however, that so far there appears little prospect of the emergence and acceptance of a completely effective security plan.

The efforts that are being pursued in the political and scientific fields ignore one fundamental factor. Man is apt to imagine that all progress and achievement is the result of his own effort and of the application of his own mind. This is a gross misconception. Such misconceptions have in the past urged powerful nations on to their ruin. We should, therefore, earnestly seek to avoid the same fate befalling us in consequence of a similar error.

A prominent Moslem statesman, Sir Zafrullah served on the Supreme Court of India before the partition which made separate countries of India and Pakistan. He subsequently became Pakistan's Minister of Foreign Affairs and Chief of Pakistan's delegation to the United Nations. In 1954 he became a judge on the International Court of Justice at the Hague.

The truth is that God is the source of all knowledge and all power. His knowledge is all-embracing: His power extends over everything. As the Koran says: "Man comprehends not anything of His knowledge save such as He wills: His authority extends over the heavens and the earth"; that is to say over the material as well as the spiritual. To quote the Koran again: "With God are unlimited treasures of all things; He reveals and bestows them as He determines."

When man acquires a fragment of this knowledge he often thinks that he comprehends all that can be known on the subject. Yet how often has not this error been exposed in the past, and how often has not the realization come that the sum total of human knowledge is but a drop out of the limitless ocean of divine knowledge? That is why we have been taught constantly to pray for increase of knowledge.

But the question remains: Whatever the ultimate source of knowledge may be, how is man to safeguard himself against its misuse and abuse? The release of atomic energy through fission or fusion may be, no doubt is, a divine bounty. How can man ensure that it shall be devoted to his service and shall not be employed for his destruction? If we truly believe that all knowledge is from God, as undoubtedly it is, then we must also believe that whenever any advance in or increase of knowledge becomes, through its misuse or abuse, a threat to human progress or security, God will also reveal the means to safeguard His creatures against such misuse or abuse. No doubt He chastens and chastises—but He has proclaimed that His mercy embraces all things.

Thus the real remedy for the grave ills and calamities that threaten is to put ourselves in accord with the True Source of all knowledge and all beneficence. We must earnestly and persistently seek and solicit His guidance, so that we may be enabled to carry through that moral and spiritual revolution inside ourselves that He desires of us in this age. We would thus become qualified to devote the ever-increasing knowledge revealed to us by God and the daily augmenting forces placed by Him at our disposal to the beneficent service of man, and safeguard humanity against any attempted misuse or abuse of these forces.

We all accept the truth that God hears and answers the earnest prayers and supplications of His servants. It is written in the Koran: "Your Lord has said, 'Call upon Me and I will answer you. Surely those who disdain to do Me service shall enter the Fire, utterly abject'." Are we not confronted today with that dread prospect? No far-fetched interpretation is here needed.

God alone has the power to hear the cry of distressed humanity and to remove the evils that may afflict it. "Who but He answers the afflicted one when he calls unto Him and removes the evil and appoints you to be successors in the earth?"

Humanity is today afflicted with dire distress and desires the removal or suppression of this evil—so that men may enjoy in peace and security the abundant bounties which are now within their reach and thus become the true inheritors of the earth and of its plenty. Let them then turn to Him who alone has the power to bestow all this upon them, and let them beseech Him earnestly to open the doors of His grace and mercy unto them.

Most appropriate to man's present plight is the prayer taught by the Holy Prophet of Islam: "Oh Lord, I commit my soul into Thy care and submit my will, my designs, and my efforts to Thy will and commit my affairs into Thy hands and place my end with Thee, in trust that Thou will secure me against Thy chastisement and will admit me to Thy Grace and Mercy. Oh Lord there is no salvation save Thy salvation, and there is no security save Thy security."

The overwhelming destructive capacity of increasingly powerful weapons has brought man face to face with the realization that there is indeed no security save the security provided by God— and no shelter save the shelter afforded by God.

We recognize and believe that God is Almighty and has power over all things. What is needed is that all of us—His creatures in all lands, men and women, children, adults and those of advanced age—should turn to Him in humility and sincerity and in full faith and trust and should continuously beseech Him for guidance.   His guidance may be vouchsafed in diverse ways. He may reveal to us knowledge whereby we could either restrain the misuse and abuse of atomic forces or could safeguard ourselves against such misuse or abuse.   Or He may so incline the hearts and minds of those who have control of these weapons as to make them resolve that atomic power shall be employed solely for the beneficent service of man and shall never be employed towards his injury or destruction.   Or, again, He has it in His power to remove from the seats of power and positions of authority those who may be determined or inclined to use these forces towards the injury or destruction of man—and substitute in their places people who are true well-wishers of humanity, so that the daily expanding horizons of knowledge and sicene should cease to cause dread and fear and should become assurances and guarantees of increasing prosperity and unmeasured beneficence.

"Oh Lord, Master of the kingdom, Thou givest the kingdom to whom Thou wilt and seizest the kingdom from whom Thou wilt, Thou exaltest whom Thou wilt.   In Thy hand is all good; Thou art powerful over everything.   Thou makest darkness to pass into Light and Thou makest light to pass into darkness.   Thou bringest forth the living from the dead and Thou bringest forth the dead from the living, and Thou providest whomsoever Thou wilt without measure." (Koran, III, 25).

Let us then all utterly abjure the false gods whom we may have set up in our temples or in our hearts, and submit ourselves wholly in utter sincerity and trust to the One True God, and humbly seek His guidance and beseech Him to grant us His security.

"And our last cry is: all perfect worthiness of praise belongs to God the Lord of all the universe."

Portents and Perspectives

The hours of intense emotion which we experienced when the
news of the explosion at Hiroshima reached us are alive in our
memory. This event produced an upheaval of many established
notions, and at the same time it had its repercussions even in the
depths of our emotional being. All the generations adult at the
same time of the explosion will, so to say, bear the stamp of the
conflicting feelings and thoughts that this extraordinary phenomenon gave rise to. The physical explosion caused, as it were, a
psychic upheaval of the same magnitude.

Our first reaction was a feeling of deep anxiety caused by the
deadly potentialities of the discovery. For, even while this event
—putting an end to the most destructive war of history—was taking place, the state of international relations did not allow us the
certitude that this was actually the "last" war.

Later on, when the scientific data concerning "control" of the
atom was better known, a vast hope took shape—as speculation
regarding the manifold technical applications of the release of
atomic energy was confirmed by the progress of our knowledge.
We would be possessing, we thought, a source of energy immensely
more powerful than that which we until now had at our disposal,
enabling us to provide for the needs of a human race which had
remained immemorially, in its great majority, exposed to all the
evils engendered by want and poverty.

This gleam of hope made lighter to bear the sorrows and anxie-
ties caused by the thousands of deceptions of the Second World
War. But when I was able to consider with greater detachment

*Before emerging as one of Turkey's major political figures, Dr. Koprulu
earned an international reputation as historian and writer. His books
have called prominent attention to Turkey's poets, philosophy and history.
His political career was climaxed by his appointment as Foreign Minister
of Turkey from which post he resigned in June, 1956.*

and objectivity the problems created by the release of the atomic energy, I came to think that even the peaceful development of atomic science contained the seeds of dangers as real and serious as its utilization for military ends; that even the peaceful use of atomic energy, if we were not controlled and organized and subordinated to the realization of certain moral and political conceptions, would provoke catastrophes as terrible as those that we imagine the explosion of the atomic bomb might cause. Let me explain:

In the early times of the steam-engine, only a few minds could have foreseen the momentous consequences that the discovery of the utilization of steam would produce. One can say without exaggeration that what at first could only appear as a purely technical invention contained the seeds of social and political upheavals which radically altered the structure of modern societies and gave birth to a series of big problems which we have not yet been able to solve. The creation of big industrial capitalism and the consecutive formation of immense proletarian masses; the disappearance of the guild system as a social force; unemployment on a —till then—unknown scale; all these interrelated problems, deriving from the rapid development of mechanical industry, occurred in a comparatively very short time—and without it being possible to foresee all their magnitude and to measure the scope of their consequences. Deep and radical changes—such as those that took place during a few decades at the beginning and at the middle of the nineteenth century — had happened in the past, through secular evolutions. These changes, in national communities, created problems which soon assumed a disquieting gravity. Another disequilibrium, causing as much concern, took place in the relations among nations. The machine further broadened the gap that already existed in technical progress between the western countries and the ancient civilizations of Asia; and a new, industrial and imperialist form of colonialism took shape. On the other hand, the diffusion of communist doctrine took a subversive and threatening form, especially after the war of 1914-1918. One of the consequences of the Second World War was to bring the

communist danger to a maximum point: the communist threat is
world-wide today, as we all know. So many social and political
problems were brought forth in a lapse of time, historically very
short. The human race has paid a high price for the mistakes
made by letting new forces evolve without control and direction.
We are still carrying on, in the social and political fields, the
liquidation of these problems which—through lack of foresight,
experience and wisdom—we failed to master in time.

History does not necessarily repeat itself. Civilizations change
and each of them has its own form. But as human reality does
not change, history offers us a lesson as regards the solution of
social problems created by changing material conditions. The
revolution of the material conditions of our world, heralded by the
discovery of atomic energy, will very probably occur at a rhythm
much faster and more disconcerting than that of the technical
revolution inaugurated by the discovery of the steam-engine; and
we can foresee that this revolution will produce social and political
problems not less serious and difficult. But cannot we hope that,
using the historical experience which our civilization has gained
at such a high price through all its tribulations during a century,
we will be able to overcome these difficulties in time?

This is how, in my opinion, the problem of the atomic age
should be considered: I want to dwell on the fact that the moral
and social and political aspects of the problem dominate its scientific and technical aspects—or should dominate, I should say, for
we cannot foresee with certitude whether they will really do so.
To technical problems, technical solutions could always be worked
out—but it is necessary that the technical solutions should be envisaged within the framework of a social and political program
and that they should fit smoothly into adequate social and political
solutions.

It is no doubt difficult today to form an idea of the progress
which will be achieved by atomic technology during the second

half of this century. But it is urgent that scientists bring together all the scientific data they possess and let us know their previsions. It is necessary that all those who play a part in the guidance of humanity should proceed at once to evolve the moral, social and political frames of the new transformation which is in sight.

Man was not aware of the problems which sprang up from the Industrial Revolution until these problems had created situations fraught with danger. On the threshold of the atomic age, we should act in such a way as to be able to enter the new era fully conscious of all the consequences of guiding it towards the realization of the moral values upon which rests all real civilization.

A certain doctrine called "dialectical materialism" contends that the formation and the evolution of these values are subordinated to the determinism of technological progress: it was stated almost a century ago that the "contradictions" created by the Industrial Revolution would cause the violent overthrow of the civilization which had given birth to them. The followers of this creed still rely on a final cataclysm which, by provoking the collapse of capitalist society, will bring forth the disappearance of these values and at the same time liquidate these contradictions. But our civilization resolves these contradictions by transforming itself socially, and has thus saved the moral values on which it rests. It achieves this within the existing national communities, by introducing greater justice in the distribution of labor and profits; in the international field, by elaborating equality of each human group, and through which each of them may gain a free access to the resources of the earth.

The realization of this immense program of material, social and political rehabilitation is for our civilization a question of moral conviction. It founds its action on the belief in human liberty, on the innate and inviolable rights of Man and in the duties of human brotherhood which derive from them. Those who have faith in these values cannot believe that the necessary solutions would come to us all ready, thanks to the historical "unfolding" of a so-called "dialectical process"—a purely metaphysical conception of which the history of recent times has sufficiently shown the fallacy;

they cannot admit that the misfortunes which we had to suffer were historically unavoidable. All the more so, as the solutions foreseen by this doctrine imply the destruction of moral values which belong to the very essence of civilization. I belong to a school of thought which believes in the free will of Man—and I am convinced that we can succeed in laying the foundations of a new civilization, an atomic civilization, on the eternal moral values which have their roots in human conscience.

If we know how to use our historical experience, we can successfully prevent the enormous power which control of atomic energy will confer on us from creating differences among nations or groups of nations. If we can succeed in organizing the development of atomic industry in a spirit of justice and human solidarity in such a way as to put its immense resources at the disposal of all the inhabitants of the earth—if we can do that, we would have in fact laid the foundations of a new civilization, in which many of the discords created by problems inherited from the past will be solved in a greater harmony of objectives and intentions.

I wish to conclude these few remarks of a general nature by quoting an observation of the French philosopher Bergson, which I think worthy to be meditated upon. Bergson observes that the complications and the increasing power of modern techniques "have given to our organism an extension so vast and a power so formidable that surely nothing of the sort had been foreseen in the structural creation of our species." Then Bergson remarks that "in this exceedingly overgrown body, the soul remains what it was, too small to fill it, too weak to guide it"; and he concludes that "this overgrown body requires a supplement of soul." This thought, formulated about forty years ago, assumes a deeper meaning today as we are facing the prospects of a technology incomparably more powerful than that of the machine era. I believe that the survival of civilization as we understand it depends, on the whole, on this "increase of soul" which we need to master this new world.

The Path of Wisdom

HIDEKI YUKAWA

Through the progress of science we have succeeded in understanding rationally the world outside the human being. In this outer world is included even the human body itself. But at the same time, with the progress of science, it has become more and more clearly recognized that in this outer world there remain things unknown and not yet understood rationally to us human beings. In this sense, we are living in an *open world*. On the contrary, however, it is apt to be neglected or completely forgotten that the inner world—or so-called spiritual world—of human beings is also an open world in a similar sense.

When we consider these matters, we may understand better the new meaning of the Freudian idea. It is obvious that unless it reaches consciousness, it cannot be the object of our rational thinking. And for that very reason it is all the more important to recognize that we are living in an open world both inwardly and outwardly. But as long as we stay at the stage of analyzing of the worlds outside and inside separately from each other, and disregard the close connection with each other, our point of view remains inevitably inconclusive and one-sided.

Perhaps it is a question to be discussed by psychological specialists rather than by a physicist like myself—but what I want to emphasize here is that when science unites with technology, which is closely associated with various interests of the human world, we can never confine the question to merely the rational aspect of what is called humanity. As long as physicists studied the structure of matter for its own sake, it was not necessary to question

A distinguished Japanese scientist, Dr. Yukawa was awarded the Nobel Prize for physics in 1949 for his work on the structure of the atom. He has taught and worked at the Institute for Advanced Study in Princeton and at Columbia University. At the present time he is Director of the Research Institute for Fundamental Physics at Kyoto University.

what desires they had as human beings or how they lived. It was quite all right to treat their ideas of life, other than their study, separately from their academic investigations. But from the very moment when nuclear physics reached the stage which made possible the practical use of atomic energy, it became impossible to discuss their way of living and thinking as scientists separately from their way of living and thinking in other respects. It became impossible to say that whatever use atomic energy might be put to, it is none of the business of scientists themselves. The case of nuclear physicists is one of the most remarkable examples, but in very many cases the problem of ethics or morals more or less comes into our consideration when science has begun to have utility. Hitherto, the progress of science had a tendency to break down rather than to promote the formation and development of the image of a man as an integration of various aspects of humanity. The division of science into many branches produced many specialists with reliable and detailed knowledge and techniques. As the kinds of machines mankind devised increased, each of them became more elaborate. Men who used them could not help evading the difficulty of understanding fully the mechanism of these machines and were satisfied with just using them because they were useful. The man who believes that he commands machines is changing into a creature who cannot live without their assistance. It is nice that machines replace human beings in various functions and reinforce and expand what man does—but we must be aware of what will happen if we let machines more and more perform the function of the human intellect.

We cannot say there is no danger that these various tendencies might accumulate and lead us to lose the unity of various aspects of humanity, and finally to end in the entire loss of humanity. We may also not be able to deny that such a breakdown might deprive mankind of human happiness. Nowadays, it is often questioned whether or not science makes men happy—but it is no easy task to answer it with confidence. Not to speak of the people of the 19th century, it is impossible for us who happen to live in the

20th century to say definitely that science always makes men happy.

There is no assurance that the progress of science will always make men happy. Science is an expression of human efforts to exploit the unknown world which is always open to our inquiry and to the discovery of new possibilities for mankind. What is there in the unknown world? There is no guarantee that the discovery of new possibilities will always make men happy. It may be the discovery of a possibility for happiness and prosperity, or it may be the discovery of a possibility for the ruination of mankind or the loss of humanity.

What on earth is human happiness? It is exceedingly difficult to answer this question properly. Can there be any branch of science that answers it directly? It even seems that human happiness cannot be the object of study. Human emotions such as joy, anger, fear and grief spring from the bottom of our mind. And in many cases it is beyond human consciousness or introspection. Man has in himself many things which he had before he became *homo sapiens*. He has them, no matter whether he perceives them or not. And human emotion is closely connected with them. Therefore, when you question human happiness it is very difficult to answer it by science alone. Everyone has something that cannot be solved rationally. And human emotion, and likewise human happiness, is bound up inseparably with these insoluble things.

Why is it that in the human world things which seem desirable and theoretically correct cannot be easily realized, while things very controversial are often realized? It is because man is not motivated merely by rational thinking or reflection. Nevertheless, this does not mean that we human beings can make little use of reason or the ability of rational thinking that we have. On the contrary, we can bring into the sphere of rational thinking a broader range of humanity by "refloating" various things sunk deeply in the bottom of our mind—or, in other words, by having our reason deepen itself and dive deeper into the bottom. With such an effort we hope to move on in the direction of saving mankind from the loss or destruction of humanity in the coming world. Isn't this the wisdom of those who live in the new era?

Moving Science Toward the Equator

NELSON ROCKEFELLER

Throughout the nineteenth century, and during most of the first half of the twentieth, the frontiers of scientific and technological inquiry and the frontiers of dynamic economic progress have been confined essentially to the world's areas of temperate climate. Over a period of some hundred and fifty years, there has been a profound revolution in the health, longevity, productivity, patterns of industrial organization and general living levels of almost all temperate zone people—with China the only major important exception.

With few and very recent qualifications, there had been no comparable change in the level or rate of progress in material well-being of the more than one billion (thousand million) inhabitants of the tropics—a term that embraces most of the territory of Africa, Latin America, the Middle East, Oceania, and South and Southeast Asia. In general, the citizen of the tropical areas must get along with two-thirds as much food, one-fourth as much cloth, one-sixth as much medical service, one-half as many teachers, and one-twentieth of the mechanical energy that is available to the average inhabitant of the industrialized West. His average income is one-tenth as high, his life expectancy one-half as long and his chance of attaining literacy fifty percent lower. It is hardly surprising that theories have been developed by a number of scholars that seek to establish a causal relationship between temperate climate and human vigor and progress, and between tropical environments and stultification of development.

If we accepted the thesis that social progress was irrevocably

An outstanding authority on the practical aspects of technical cooperation between nations, Mr. Rockefeller has served in public office under three Presidents. He has played a major role in the development of programs designed to help people abroad understand and use American know-how.

determined by climate, the world's political prospects would be grim indeed; for there is compelling evidence that human aspirations for progressive improvement are not confinable within any zones of latitude.

It is significant, I think, that the great cycle of progress in Western Europe and North America following the industrial revolution stemmed from the renaissance of scientific investigation and its application to the problems of those areas. The long history of the rise and fall of past civilizations adequately refutes the suggestion that either intellectual attainment or genius for social organization is restricted to any one race or area of the world's surface. The content and method of science have universal application; and I am firmly convinced that once they are adapted to the problems of tropical environments, the results there will be entirely comparable to what has been achieved in areas that are not conclusively more amenable to human use because their mean temperatures happen to be lower.

Within the time allotted, I can do no more than offer a few suggestions of lines of progress that may open as science and technology are brought to bear upon areas nearer the equator.

I am sure that one major requisite is the improvement of health in the tropics. In many tropical countries only one-half of the children born reach the productive age of 15—which means that there is an appalling disparity between the number of bodies that can work and the stomachs that must be fed. The prevailing incidence of such mass diseases as malaria, hookworm, yaws, bilharziasis, and trachoma; of such pestilential diseases as cholera, smallpox, yellow fever, the typhoids and plague; of nutritional deficiency ailments like beri beri, pellagra, rickets, scurvy and anemia—these drag down the level of intellectual and physical vigor of those who survive to adulthood.

All of these are commonly termed "tropical diseases", but it is noteworthy that virtually all of them were once rampant in the temperate zones as well. The application of science through organized *preventive medicine* is bringing them under control in the tropics too, and it is a noteworthy and heartening fact that the preventive medicine programs most urgently needed in the tropics cost only about one-tenth as much per capita as the "corrective medicine" programs now sustained in the industrialized areas of the temperate zones. There is, for example, reason to believe that a concerted international effort and the expenditure of perhaps an additional $20 million over a few years' period might serve completely to eradicate malaria—the disease that presently blights the health of something like 300 million of the world's people.

Agriculture is a second major field in which scientific investigation and application promise to achieve revolutionary improvement in tropical economies. It is true that compared to temperate zone achievements, yields per acre in the tropics are generally low. It is equally true that over large areas of the tropics there are formidable problems of soil poverty, leaching from heavy rainfall, and difficulties in employment of mechanical equipment due to terrain and the mire of tropical rainy seasons. Other tropical areas suffer from lack of sufficient rainfall or sources of irrigation water, or from alkalinity that irrigation may even intensify. There are numerous records of failure in the direct application of techniques that have been marvelously effective in the temperate zones, to tropical conditions to which they are entirely inapplicable.

Yet there is every reason to believe that science, once it is brought to bear directly upon the problems of *tropical agriculture*, will achieve just as spectacular results as it has in North America and Western Europe—where yields per acre and per agricultural worker have been increased many fold, and where large areas once classified as waste land are now rated in the highest bracket of fertility.

It is possible to chart a variety of lines through which the knowledge and procedures now being developed in our agricultural schools, and in our chemistry and physics laboratories, can vastly improve the agriculture output of the tropics. I can state them with more assurance, since many of them have been tested in practice through the work of the IBEC Research Institute with which I have been associated.

We have found that the first requirement is the systematic analysis of tropical soils to determine their virtues and deficiencies, area by area and plot by plot.

We have demonstrated that through improved agricultural methods—including proper fertilizer applications, determined by scientific experimentation to balance costs against increased yields —corn production in Venezuela and Brazil can be raised to as much as 100 bushels per acre as against the 20 to 25 bushel production under existing practices.

In Brazil, we have been distributing upon a large scale varieties of hybrid corn seed that have produced for the local farmers 50 to 60 bushels per acre—under drought conditions that have resulted in virtually complete crop failure to plantings of the open-pollinated varieties commonly employed. Under all conditions, these hybrids have consistently outperformed all other seed types of corn in use in the area.

Even more impressive are the experiments we have been carrying out with the new herbicide chemicals "2, 4D" and "2, 4, 5T" —as well as the dinitro phenols applied after the seeding but before the sprouting of corn and other cereal crops.

New chemicals have shown results that promise to revolutionize the tropical farmers' perennial and often losing battle against the weeds that choke off food-crop production.

In Venezuela, IBEC Research Institute has shown that chemical sprays of the hormone type can be used with similar effectiveness to keep down brush infestation in pastures. In areas where all previous systems have failed—where attempts to chop out or uproot woody plant growth in pastureland hardly kept up with new sproutings of brush and thorn—these new chemicals have proved able to do the job and have substantially raised the cattle-carrying capacity of previously unproductive pastureland.

Other chemical sprays can bring about earlier and more nearly uniform maturation of rice, with indications that similar results may be obtained with other crops and with a consequent reduction of losses from a variety of causes; and a whole family of new chemicals—aldrin, dieldrin and endrin—non-toxic to humans but lethal to insects—has effectively cut down insect damage to food crops—damage that is a universal problem, but particularly vexing in tropical environments.

I have cited the above lines of progress which convince me that tropical agriculture is on the threshold of revolutionary progress. But these by no means exhaust the potentials that are being developed in the world's chemical and physics laboratories. One of the newest miracles of modern research, the radioactive tracer element, promises to offer swift and sure knowledge of the amount of nutrition actually absorbed by crops of various kinds from soils, fertilizers and mulches. It promises to be a key instrument in exploring what is still largely the no-man's land of tropical agricultural possibilities.

In these, and many other ways, the "frontiers of knowledge" are moving toward the equator, and promise to bring new hope and new achievement to the more than a billion human personalities that live in tropical environments. I am confident that improvement of health and agricultural procedures in these areas will be accompanied by a general broadening and improvement of other segments of their economies, as has occurred in temperate zone societies.

Pure and applied science may well be our most valuable export, but it certainly is one that we can send abroad with least cost to ourselves. The usefulness of science is not bounded by imaginary latitude lines upon the globe. It is for those nations most advanced in science to help spread its benefits to others and thereby promote humanity's hopes for the future.

The Promise of the Atom

HOMI BHABHA

In a broad view of human history, it is possible to discern three great epochs. The first is marked by the emergence of the early civilizations in the valleys of the Euphrates, the Indus, and the Nile; the second by the industrial revolution, leading to the civilization in which we live; and the third by the discovery of atomic energy and the dawn of the atomic age, which we are just entering.

In a practical sense, energy is the great prime mover, which makes possible the multitude of actions on which our life depends. Indeed, it makes possible life itself.

Now, as to the first epoch . . . Man has existed on this earth for well over 250,000 years. And yet the earliest civilizations of which we have record only date back some 8,000 years. It took man several hundred thousand years to acquire those skills and techniques on which the early civilizations were based—agriculture, animal husbandry, weaving, pottery, brick-making and metallurgy. The acquisition of these techniques and the emergence of the early civilizations must be regarded as the first great epoch in human history.

Despite many differences in habit, culture and social pattern, all these early civilizations were built essentially on the same foundation. All the energy for doing mechanical work, for tilling the ground, for drawing water, for carrying loads, for locomotion, was supplied by human or animal muscle. Chemical energy—as, for example, that obtained by burning wood—was used only for cooking and heating and, to a limited extent, in metallurgy.

It is important to note the severe limitations that this restricted

One of India's most distinguished atomic scientists, Dr. Bhabha was the Chairman of the first International Conference on the Peaceful Uses of Atomic Energy, held in Geneva in 1955. He has been the Chairman of India's Department of Atomic Energy since 1947 and Director of the Tata Institute of Fundamental Research since 1945.

supply of energy puts on the development of civilization. A man in the course of heavy physical labor in an eight hour day can turn out about half a kilowatt-hour of useful work. This is not much more than is necessary to maintain him at a bare subsistence level. It is to be compared with the rough figure of twenty kilowatt hours or more of energy per person which is daily utilized in the industrially advanced countries today. It follows that a high level of physical comfort and culture could only be enjoyed by a small fraction of the population by making use of the collected surplus labor of the rest. It is sometimes forgotten that all the ancient civilizations were carried on the muscle power of slaves or of a particular class of society. Through the very limitations of the available energy, the fruits of civilization could only be enjoyed by a few.

A departure from this basic pattern began only with the scientific and technical developments of the seventeenth and eighteenth centuries. The widespread use of chemical energy—especially that obtained by burning the fossil fuels, coal and oil—marks the second great epoch of human history. It led to the industrialized pattern of society which is typical of this age. In one highly industrialized country today 23 kilowatt-hours of energy are utilized daily per person, corresponding to the muscular effort of 45 slaves. In another advanced country the figure is about twice this.

The total consumption of energy in the world has gone up in a staggering manner. To illustrate, let us use the letter "Q" to stand for the energy derived from burning some thirty-three thousand million tons of coal. In the eighteen and a half centuries after Christ, the total energy consumed averaged less than $\frac{1}{2}Q$ per century. But by 1850, the rate had risen to one Q per century. Today, the rate is about ten Q per century.

One reason for the staggering increase in the consumption of energy, of course, is that the population of the world has been increasing rapidly. It is estimated to have been a few hundred million in one A.D., to have reached 1500 million in 1900, 2000 million in 1930 and about 2300 million in 1950. Experts estimate that it will be between 3500 and 5000 million by the end of this century—in under 50 years.

But the per capita consumption of energy has also been increasing at about 2 or 3 percent per annum. And it can be expected to increase still more rapidly as the underdeveloped areas of the world, with their large populations, become industrialized.

Now, of the enormous consumption of energy in the world today, about 80% is provided by the combustion of coal, oil and gas. Hydro-electric power provides less than one and one-half per cent and is never likely to contribute more than a small fraction of the total energy consumed in the world. Hence, as the total demand increases, a larger and larger fraction will have to be provided by the fossil fuels, coal and oil—unless some entirely new source of energy is found. But it is probable that, at the rate at which the world consumption of energy is increasing, these reserves will be exhausted in under a century. We are exhausting these reserves, which have been built up by nature over some 250,000,000 years, in a few centuries—in a flash of geological time.

All these facts point to the absolute necessity of finding some new source of energy, if the light of our civilization is not to be extinguished because we have burnt out our fuel reserves.

And so we turn to atomic energy for a solution. For the full industrialization of the underdeveloped countries, for the continuation of our civilization and its further development, atomic energy is not merely an aid; it is an absolute necessity. The acquisition by Man of the knowledge of how to release and use atomic energy must be recognized as the third great epoch in human history.

There is little doubt that many atomic power stations will be established in different parts of the world during the next ten years. But the historical period we are just entering, in which atomic energy released by the fission process will supply some of the power requirements of the world, may well be regarded one day as the primitive period of the atomic age. It is well known that atomic energy can also be obtained by a fusion process, as in the hydrogen bomb. I venture to predict that a method will be found for liberating fusion energy in a controlled manner within the next two decades. When that happens, the energy problems of the world will truly have been solved forever—for the fuel will be as plentiful as the heavy hydrogen in the oceans.

All the basic discoveries upon which atomic energy is based were made before the Second World War by scientists of many nations working in free and full collaboration. The war put an end to this free exchange of knowledge, and most of the technical developments concerning atomic energy were made subsequently by a few nations, each working in isolation behind a wall of secrecy. The International Atoms for Peace Conference held in Geneva in August, 1955, as the result of the bold initiative of President Eisenhower, has already broken down many of these barriers. The exchange of knowledge in the field of atomic energy has been maintained. And recently a leading Russian scientist described at Harwell the remarkable work that has been done in the Soviet Union to harness atomic energy from fusion, thus breaking down another barrier of secrecy. We can hope with some justification that the barriers which remain will gradually disappear altogether.

Speeded on its way by international cooperation and the free exchange of knowledge, the ever-widening dawn of the atomic age promises for people everywhere in the world a life fuller and happier than anything we can visualize today.

New Patterns of Society

WILLIAM O. DOUGLAS

Two problems will be of cardinal importance in the field of law during the second half of the twentieth century.

The first is the molding of democratic constitutions to fit the needs of subjugated peoples emerging from colonialism and developing within these countries democratic habits and institutions.

Formulating democratic constitutions for nations newly emerging into independence is not a difficult task. Creating democratic institutions and instilling democratic habits is much more difficult. Most of these new nations have little or no demorcratic tradition. People of different cultures, religions, and languages must often be unified under a single government. Preservation of liberty and equality for diverse groups and minorities is no easy matter. It is one thing to write concepts of freedom into a constitution; it is another thing to make the constitution a living creed. But it can be done as proved by the experience of India.

Consider the magnitude of the obstacles facing the new Indian democracy at the time of its birth in 1947. Nine Governors' Provinces had been under a modified form of democratic rule since 1937. By contrast, some 560 Indian states had been under the autocratic rule of hereditary princes. Moreover, India is a nation of 17 different languages and several hundred different dialects. It has many different religious groups; and it was long saddled by a caste system that the new Constitution outlawed. Unification of such a nation was a real challenge to the political leadership of India.

Under Nehru, the leaders met the challenge. They fashioned

An Associate Justice of the Supreme Court of the United States with wide ranging interests, Justice Douglas is an inveterate observer of other lands and their problems. What he has seen on his extensive and continuing foreign travels are recorded in his many books.

the many states into a working federalism of 15 units. Local and
national leaders united to make this new machinery work smoothly.
An independent judiciary saw to it that individual rights were not
sacrificed and that discrimination was outlawed. Education of
the masses in their political responsibilities was vigorously under-
taken. The general elections in 1951 showed that even illiterate
people are intelligent and can act responsibly.

The Indian Constitution is a fountainhead of democratic freedoms. The dignity and worth of the individual are constitutional
keystones. India adheres to the creed of democracy. The Pre-
amble states that the purpose of the Constitution is to secure to all
India's citizens:

"*Justice*, social, economic and political;

"*Liberty* of thought, expression, belief, faith and worship;

"*Equality* of status and of opportunity; and to promote among
them all

"*Fraternity* assuring the dignity of the individual and the unity
of the Nation."

The manner in which the Constitution is being applied and
interpreted in India has made these noble goals powerful forces
in the nation.

Burma, Ceylon, and Pakistan have made great strides forward
under new constitutions that are fresh embodiments of the spirit
of liberty. Indonesia, Morocco, and Vietnam are moving in the
same direction. The spirit of freedom, so strongly demonstrated
at Bandung, is now a powerful political force shaping the constitutions and political habits of peoples long subjugated. It will be
a major force in world affairs during the balance of this century
as other nations gain their independence.

Our second major problem in the field of law is an agreement
by all nations on a body of principles for the control of nuclear
power. The successful resolution of this problem is imperative
to the survival of mankind.

This age of bombs with a destructive force measured in mega-
tons presents man with the gravest problem in his history. The
force that is capable of destroying all civilization must be sub-

jected to a body of law applicable to all people in all nations.

Man, with all his ingenuity at work, has in the past ten years taken some pioneer steps toward meeting this challenge. A number of proposals for the international control of nuclear power have been advanced. In 1946 the Acheson-Lilienthal plan was presented. It was adopted in substance by the United Nations Atomic Energy Commission and became known as the UN Majority Plan. It was a bold plan. It called for a single international commission which would have ownership of all dangerous nuclear facilities and materials—from the mines to electric power stations. There would be sweeping inspection arrangements designed to detect secret production facilities. This plan proved to be unacceptable to the Soviet Union, but it showed what man's inventive genius in the field of law can achieve.

After the Acheson-Lilienthal plan there followed a number of disarmament proposals. The United Nations Disarmament Commission was organized. And in 1953 President Eisenhower announced his Atoms for Peace plan. He called for an international pool of fissionable material for research and development of the peaceful uses of atomic energy. While not a program for control of nuclear power, the Atoms for Peace plan manifested a spirit of cooperation which is essential to an effective plan of international control. And at Geneva in 1955 the President advanced his "open skies" plan of aerial inspection and exchange of military blueprints. This plan would reduce the temptation of atomic or thermonuclear attack by eliminating the element of surprise. The "open skies" plan would be a preliminary step to disarmament and international control.

The international control of nuclear power is a difficult problem. But it must be solved. Confidence built by cooperation is a sound beginning.

Whither Mankind?

HALIDE EDIP ADIVAR

The frontiers of knowledge and humanity's hopes for the future may appear, at first, as two different subjects, demanding treatment from different angles. Yet as one begins to consider them, though separately, one realizes the influence of the one on the other in their different aspects.

Have we reached or can we ever reach the frontiers of knowledge?

So far all the most miraculous achievements of science have had their roots in the discoveries of a handful of geniuses. There is no doubt that intellectual as well as metaphysical curiosity played their part in these discoveries. In applying these discoveries to life, undoubtedly the desire to ease human suffering, to find a way to human well-being, was also an important factor. This desire naturally had a connection with the hopes of humanity for the future.

In trying to diminish the time factor within or between nations we find ourselves on the verge of realizing contact with the moon or the other worlds sooner than we expected. All this has created, if not in the great artists themselves, at least in the ordinary man, a vanity which is very much like a divinity complex. One feels in the attitudes of shallow thinkers of today a reptetition of the eighteenth or early nineteenth century mentality which is expressed in the thought: "Man can do everything!"

The forward march of scientific knowledge has also led to a wider application of its power over life—which is seen in the un-

A noted Turkish writer and educator, Professor Adivar is well known to the people of India and the United States, countries in which she has taught Turkish literature and philosophy. Since 1939 she has been a professor of English literature at the University of Istanbul. Her books— among them "Islam", "Turkey Faces West", and "Conflict Between East and West"—have been widely translated outside of Turkey.

imaginably wide mechanization of human life and labor.   The results have been manifold and at times contradictory.

One aspect of this super mechanization, leading to automation, was originally due to the desire to ease human labor and procure leisure.   But leisure that takes away a definite amount of daily work and, with it, the necessary sense of duty, is the first step toward the general degeneration of mankind.   It has also diminished the creative urge in man, because anything that does not deal with industry or the machine has lost its value in our time.

Let us now review the pros and cons of this onward march of mechanization.   The urge to kill time and to occupy the leisure of the masses finds a realistic representation in Aldous Huxley's book, "Brave New World".   On the other hand, the advance of scientific knowledge is conquering disease and lengthening human life in a way hitherto unimagined and unknown.   It naturally leads to a tremendous increase of world population and if it continues at this rate and automation becomes general, there will be little or no space for humans to move about in.

The onward march of human knowledge, seen from any angle, plays a dominant part in shaping the hopes of humanity and intensifying that curiosity, which all men have, to a greater or lesser degree.   When this curiosity—based on the eternal wonder of man's mind confronted by the mystery of creation—will reach its frontiers, it is impossible to foretell.   However, it seems to be impossible to solve the great mystery of life, even when we can travel by air and create contact with other worlds, such as the Moon and Mars.   After-life remains an eternal mystery.

But this ceaseless endeavor to increase knowledge will proceed toward two goals: to increase discoveries which will create further mechanical gadgets and do away with human labor; to create a robot population which will mean an eternal leisure for the naturally born human beings.   At the same time, the discovery of new weapons is bound to create a different mentality towards war. Mass-murder will be carried on from laboratories and through bombs directed by robots.   The country which has the ablest scientists will be able to destroy the entire population of rival countries.

It may in the end lead to the disappearance of our globe. Who knows whether it has not already happened to other globes in this great universe?

Within nations the use of leisure, without degeneration, is another subject of scientific study. The responsibility of man towards his kind at the moment when the world has attained such an advanced stage of progress, should make one stop and consider the next step. The ultimate desire of man is to find the right way to a better future, but so far the desire has not produced a satisfactory result.

There seems to be a general unconscious urge to enjoy life and get the best of it. That is why, perhaps, one hears so many different opinions on the subject of the frontiers of knowledge and humanity's hope for the future. I will mention only one, which is both amusing and food for thought. Someone asked, "Whither are we going . . . where will our power-complex lead us?" And another repeated the legend of Nimrod which we had all heard as children, half a century ago.

"My conception of the world of today is this: In our childhood we used to hear the legend of Nimrod, the builder of the tower of Babel. He must have been a first rate genius for he posed as the most powerful god on earth. According to the legend he found the means to fly to heaven and he flew up with the aim of dethroning Almighty God and taking his place. As he flew (in whatever plane it was!), a tiny mosquito entered his brain and so annoyed him that Nimrod was obliged to have his head constantly beaten with a cudgel. Finally his head was broken into pieces and he died."

Well, the frontiers of knowledge will never be reached on this side of creation, but the divinity complex which has created Nimrods in the past, will multiply them into thousands, each trying to fly higher and to break the heads of the others. Eventually when we believe that we have reached the frontiers, our world may be destroyed by the rival Nimrods in their effort to overcome each other and in their efforts to dethrone the Almighty in Heaven.

Our Changing Communications

LEE DE FOREST

The first half of this twentieth century has seen the magnificent completion of a program of technical and scientific progress in the fields of communications. Technology has opened new vistas for man's energies, ambitions and accomplishment which have vastly surpassed the wildest imaginations of the scientists of the nineteenth century. By the same token, we, of this present era, are not justified in attempting to foresee the measure of the magnitude of what our sons and our grandsons may be enabled, in their turn, to achieve.

Already, the first half of this century has seen broadcasting— once a novelty—enlarge from one single small transmitter station to more than 5,000, spread all over the face of the earth.

I have, of course, watched with intense personal interest the influence of the electron tube upon our modern civilization. Eminent scientists, such as Charles Kettering and Nobel Prize Winner Isadore Rabi have, indeed, likened this tube, because of its epoch-making achievements, to the ancient discovery of the wheel, or the earlier use of fire in speeding the evolution of upward climbing Mankind.

But is is certain that I can claim no such conception of the unforeseen evolutionary, revolutionary achievements of this simple-appearing invention. Let it suffice at this time merely to call attention to what the 3-electrode tube and its descendants have made possible in spreading over the entire face of the globe an invisible network of international, inter-continental, telephonic communication, whereby the ancient barriers of unlike languages no longer

Popularly known as "the Father of Electronics", Mr. de Forest has made many notable contributions in this field. His invention of the vacuum tube in 1906 resulted in the development of modern radio broadcasting. His ingenuity also made possible radar and television.

persist. Coupled with this all important development comes now radio's sister development, television, linking distant sight with the voice.

Already in the U.S. are in daily use more than 30 million television receivers, a number daily increasing by leaps and bounds. Great Britain is following as are other nations in Europe and Latin America. By adroit location of relay stations and by taking advantage of reflections from the ionosphere, trans-ocean television is only a matter of, say, 10 years or less.

I am much more conservative in my estimate of interspace flight! True, this year may become known as the year of the first man-made planet—the tiny artificial earth-satellite. But to place a man in a multi-stage rocket and project him into the controlling gravitational field of the moon, where the passenger can make scientific observation, perhaps land alive, and then return to earth —all that costitutes a wild dream worthy of Jules Verne.

But why not rather limit his greatest efforts to improvement of the existing conditions on earth? Here, surely, his countless problems, humanistic as well as scientific, demand our immediate and most earnest effort to solve.

And in communications, radio can and is being used as a practical means for the gradual elimination of inter-racial, international human barriers. Foremost in this battle stand such splendid institutions as the Voice of America, Radio Free Europe, and similar undertakings. An only casual observation of the elaborately organized efforts of these institutions has amazed me, and would similarly astonish millions of Americans who generously contribute toward the daily maintenance of their activities, but who unfortunately cannot grasp any adequate comprehension of the intensive, carefully planned, business-like procedures of these radio agencies, so vitally important in the Crusade for Freedom.

Already information leaking to the West from the communist controlled "captive" nations is encouraging devoted men and women who, 24 hours each day, are broadcasting across the Iron Curtain, both by the ether and by the upper air-currents, news and every form of encouragement to the millions now cruelly captured and forcibly dominated, a process which will eventually, inevitably enable them to regain their former freedoms.

That blessed day is coming, as surely as the bright sunlight beams upon their lands, even as now the rays of radio work both day and night to hasten its final dawn.

Prospects for Stability

W. J. GIBBONS

Certain conclusions quickly become evident from even cursory study of the present state of world agriculture. About two-thirds of the people of the world still lack balanced diets considered desirable for good health and economic and intellectual efficiency. The same number of people—usually the same ones—have a great need for increased consumption of agricultural products in the form of clothing, newsprint, housing. It is sobering to realize that hundreds of millions in the world today regularly subsist on diets so deficient that health and vitality are seriously impaired.

Only through considerable economic development can the people of the underdeveloped regions of the world be better fed, better clothed and better housed. Without it they will go from bad to worse, as additional population makes demands on a static or near static economy.

But unfortunately, certain popular writers, and some others who should know better, have spoken of the present world food problem as if it were solely or primarily one of population. Admittedly, much of the distress results from pressures of growing populations upon economic resources. It does not follow, as the pessimists imply, that the world can no longer feed its people and that the Malthusian dilemma is upon us. To the extent that such writers and spokesmen have focused attention on the very important population factor in the food-to-people relationship, they have done some good. But by and large the population pessimists have done us a bad turn by diverting attention from the

Professor of Economics at Loyola College in Baltimore, Father Gibbons has made outstanding contributions to the social sciences. He played an active part at the World Population Conference in 1954 and at the UNESCO National Conference in 1951.

fundamental question of how to effect economic improvement and how to increase food production to desired levels.

What the population pessimists fail to realize is that much of mankind is still struggling along on a primitive, or near primitive agriculture, and that economic development has been lacking also in fields other than agriculture. The countries and people affected are bound down by their inadequate economic structure. Even where population increase has been minor, as was the case in much of Africa until recent years, the problem of underproductivity exists because of static economic conditions.

Had all the hunting and fishing peoples of the past adopted the same attitude as the contemporary population pessimists, economic progress would have never begun. When populations began pressing upon limited hunting resources, or upon the restricted capacity of primitive agriculture, they would have despaired at the seeming impossibility of the situation. Fortunately for future generations, at least some of these primitive peoples were ingenious and enterprising enough to find new ways of raising food and producing other necessities.

There are, of course, serious obstacles to be overcome in improving the agriculture or developing the economies of the underdeveloped regions. The imparting of technical skill is slowed down by illiteracy and poverty. Men are usually reluctant to accept changes and new ways of doing things, unless they are convinced that the new situation will be better than what they are used to. Political instability makes investment of foreign capital unlikely and slows down the accumulation of domestic capital. Not a little of the potential improvement in agriculture must await reform in land tenure, electrification, the increase of rural credit facilities, the building of farm-to-market roads, and the like.

Faced with the general problem of world underproductivity and inadequate food supply, the more developed countries have initiated programs of economic development and agricultural improvement through technical and economic aid to less fortunate areas. In this development—through the assistance of individual countries and the United Nations—lies one area of hope. Within each of the underdeveloped countries, not only governmental action, but the constructive work which labor unions, farm organizations, business firms, educational institutions and other non-governmental agencies can offer points another avenue to progress.

In the long run, of course, the solution to world economic improvement is largely political. That is, considerably more cooperation among nations will be necessary—since much of the progress we look for is dependent upon freer movement of both goods and people.

But even in the short run, the prospects of immediate improvement in limited ways are quite good. It is not necessary to await modernization of the whole economy, to increase food production to a significant degree. Thus introduction of a simple steel plow in place of a digging stick, use of scythes rather than sickles, employment of mechanical pumps instead of human muscle, are all ways of saving manpower and increasing productivity. Crop outputs can be increased also by use of modern strains, like hybrid corn, by the utilization of manure for fertilizer instead of fuel, by improvements in land tenure, rural credit, restrictions upon rents, and the like. The list of immediately possible improvements could be multiplied indefinitely. The important thing, however, is to discover what improvement is most significant in a particular locality—and then to have it introduced by winning the people to its adoption. The size of the job to be done is tremendous.

Planning for Tomorrow

ARTHUR R. BURNS

It now looks as if the second world war marked the beginning of an era of widespread economic planning in the richer as well as the poorer countries. This planning is aimed at reaching objectives in the most economical way. Economists can work out some of the consequences of pursuing various courses, but governments will have the problem of choosing objectives after counting the cost of the various possible policies. Three particularly difficult choices will concern the future: size of the population, the rate at which to invest in the means of raising future output, and the extent of government intervention in economic life.

In many of the poorer countries, populations have speeded up their increase during the present century. Many (but not all) of them have so many people in relation to their resources that levels of income will fall unless the population ceases to increase. Planning for a higher level of living will fail if increases in production are all used up in supporting more people. Reducing the size of families will be difficult, however, because the available methods of control need improvement, and high rates of multiplication are deeply embedded in the mores of many countries. The first step in meeting this problem will be to convince the people that the level of living depends partly on the number of people sharing the national income. Realization of this fact is now beginning to spread and some governments have already proceeded to the second step by providing knowledge of methods of regulating family size.

Deciding how much of present income to set aside to provide for

An outstanding American economist, Dr. Burns has an unusually rich background in international economics, having been in charge of economic research studies in several countries of the world. Between projects he has been teaching economics at Columbia University since 1928.

more ample production in the future will also be a serious problem. There is no doubt that capital makes labor more productive. One of the problems of the poorer countries will be the large amount of capital they need, even in comparison with the richer countries when they began to raise their national incomes. A century or so ago the best known methods of production called for much less capital than they do now. Some economies are possible by accepting less than the most up to date equipment, but increases in output may thus be slowed. Another problem in these countries will arise from the fact that much of the capital needed in the early stages of development will be in transportation, power, and irrigation which yield benefits only slowly, although in the long run the benefits are large.

While the need for capital is great, only a small amount of present income can be diverted away from consumption into investment in a poor country. One way out will be to resort to loans and grants from other countries. If wisely used, such financing may increase production more than is necessary to service the loan. But the country must first decide whether it prefers slower development to reliance on foreign aid. Some countries have imposed restrictions on foreign investment for fear of the recurrence of past experiences of ruthless economic imperialism. In fact, however, foreign lenders and their governments seem to have become much more civilized in dealing with their poorer neighbors, and a number of governments in poorer countries are now moving towards providing more attractive conditions to foreign lenders. But planning countries will also find that the world cannot provide enough capital to export for the rapid development of all countries now anxious for economic progress. Where production does increase because of investment from either foreign or domestic sources the country must choose whether to use the added income to raise levels of living in the present, or to invest in still further future production. Yet poverty-ridden populations will press for immediate relief. They are already demanding lower land rents, higher wages, and social security. Some such reforms increase the worker's output, but they will also raise consumption and reduce possible investment. Yet to reject these claims is likely to undermine confidence in the government and in planning.

The third problem, namely that of deciding how extensive government conomic controls shall be, is likely to be serious for a number of decades. Past experience in these poorer countries, and the scale of their present problems, suggest that governments will have to be far more active than they were in Britain and the United States during their periods of intense development. But comprehensive planning of the whole economy and vigorous enforcement of plans may impede the establishment and growth of democracy. Governments would control what is to be produced and how it is to be disposed of, which means control over conditions of work, consumption and investment. Nevertheless, such planning may speed up the accumulation of capital by postponing improvements in present economic conditions.

It may be possible, however, to restrict planning to the parts of the economy in which action is most necessary to start up progress. The government may impose import duties, give subsidies, provide capital or establish government enterprises. It may obtain the needed funds by increasing taxes, shifting the burden of the tax system, or borrowing from foreign sources or international agencies. There would remain room for individual initiative, and the possibility of encouraging it. This sort of planning will succeed, however, only if the population can be persuaded that the way to better economic conditions is the way of change, which will often be painful. The richer members of the population will have to pay more taxes and make a more active contribution to production. The mass of the population will have to accept adjustments such as being parted from their land so that the land as a whole may be more efficiently used, leaving their present place and way of living to go to new places and new jobs, working under strange new conditions, and receiving less help from their children (who may spend more time at school). The governmental system will have to be more competent and incorruptible than it often is at present, because plans will have to be skillfully drawn and economically administered.

Finally, as one looks over the later decades of the century, one must ask whether efforts to raise the level of living of most of the human race are doomed to frustration because the world does not possess enough resources. Even the present population of the world needs more food, and many populations will increase as nourishment and medical services improve. The present land of the world, if used in the best ways now known, can provide a good deal more food and the ceiling on the food supply will doubtless be raised by further improvements in knowledge. But there will be a limit to the number of people who can be fed, although where the limit will be, even with the best planning, depends on future advances in knowledge. Rising levels of living, however, call for somewhat different resources such as those providing energy, more structural materials and more services. New sources of power seem to be in prospect. We are learning to make use of the more plentiful minerals and the mineral resources of the world have been only partly explored. It looks, therefore, as if higher levels of living for a not too greatly increased world population will be more attainable than decent levels for a rapidly increasing population.

In conclusion, planning is not a mechanical formula for achieving the good life in terms of material things. Economists need to know much more than they now do to draft plans that will avoid waste and error. But planning brings out into the open difficult choices that must be made before one can begin to plan. The choices made concerning population growth and willingness to make present sacrifices in the hope of a better future will express the outlook and aspirations of each country. The translation of plans into real progress will call for acceptance of change and efficient government. But, although planning is not easy, it holds great promise for the relief of poverty and inequality all over the world. And it must be remembered that the first steps are the most difficult.

Overview

WHITNEY GRISWOLD

Unity in diversity is the mainstay of a free society. Democracy tolerates controversy. It lives by consensus. The symposium just concluded provides a remarkable demonstration of these principles. Thirty-four learned and experienced men representing fifteen nations on five continents have spoken with the authority of their eminence in such varied fields as philosophy, law, government, economics, psychology, anthropology, biology, physics, technology, religion, education and literature. They have done so as individuals with complete freedom to think and say what they would under no restraint save that of truth. Their opinions form a pattern whose whole is truly the sum, not merely a collection, of its parts—a pattern that reveals so clearly both the perils and the promises of the future that the peoples of the earth could live by it if only they would allow reason to be their guide.

The world in this projection is one in which humanity's hopes and fears hang in delicate balance. Man has achieved a mastery over nature that can either bring the human race into an era of peace and plenty or destroy it. Atomic energy and technology— like the capricious deities that were supposed to hold the scales of mortal destiny in ancient mythology — can make the deserts bloom or depopulate the world. This is one major theme of the symposium. Another is the mechanical performance of human skills on a constantly ascending plane of rationality that could end either in consummation of man's long struggle for freedom or in a mere exchange of inhuman for human masters. Scientific knowledge has no theoretical limit. A century ago disease and famine were accepted as inevitable, and explained away as fate or as the postulates of deterministic philosophy. Among the contribu-

Historian and author, Dr. Griswold is the president of Yale University, the second oldest university in the United States.

tors to this symposium, and on the frontiers of knowledge upon
which they stand, nothing is inevitable save birth and death.
Science, once accused of robbing man of his free will, seems to be
giving it back to him. What will he do with it?

There is no room in this prospect for deterministic philosophy.
We are not sinners in the hands of an angry god, predestined to
suffering or servitude. Dialectical materialism has been refuted
by empirical evidence and by the very unfolding of history which
was originally claimed to support it. The industrial revolution
has not steadily diminished but steadily increased labor's share
of the wealth it produces until in the industrial countries in Western Europe and North America this share has risen to between
seventy and eighty per cent of the net national product—exactly
the opposite of what Marx and his followers predicted. Their
theory, in the words of Mr. Colin Clark, "is so flatly contradicted
by all the facts that those who propagate it must be very ignorant
men, or unfortunately, in a few cases, well-informed men who are
deliberately setting out to pervert the truth." The same could be
said of other social, economic or political theories stemming from
the frontiers of knowledge of 1857. There is no reason for us to
be frightened by the ghosts of Malthus and Marx.

It is in the direct interest of the highly industrialized western
nations to further with all energy the development of the underdeveloped and overpopulated countries of the world. It is humanity's hope that they may be able to do so. No economic
barriers stand in the way—only political barriers, composed of
pride, fear, superstition and ignorance. Colonialism is dead. With
it has died the hope of material gain from warfare. The saber-
rattler has become a clanking skeleton. In the realization of these
truths lies hope that the veils of obscurity which separate the
nations may be parted and ways of commerce and culture opened
between them. Thus atomic energy lends its influence to reason
and peace.

But fear of atomic warfare alone will not suffice. To avert
destruction and put to peaceful uses among the nations the scientific knowledge at our command we shall need more than the

stereotypes of international politics. We shall need spiritual help, the assistance of education, the wisdom of philosophy and all that reveals more truly the individual nature and aspirations of man. Fortunately we possess these means, too, and have only to make use of them. So we find ourselves at the end of the symposium looking out upon a world in which, between a balanced peril and hope, the symposium itself tips the scales in favor of hope. It is as creative an opportunity for the human imagination as ever emerged from the frontiers of knowledge in any generation.

To take advantage of it we must not allow that imagination to be inhibited by fear or shackled by dogma. We must give it freedom. We must educate it. We must employ it. As we do so we shall discover, with the authors of this symposium, that as humanity is united in its hopes it can be united in its fulfillment. We scoff at the fears that obsessed mankind five hundred years ago— the supernatural monsters, the jumping-off places—as products of the imagination. Yet it was this same imagination that produced the scientific tknowledge which put these fantasies to flight. Our fears in 1957 are no less a product of our imagination than those of 1457—and the same imagination that has created them in their atomic image is capable of saving us from them, exactly as it has done in the past. This, I think, is the ultimate message of our symposium. It comes supported by such learning and unanimity of feeling from so many nations that humanity's hopes for the future may well become humanity's achievement — and the frontiers of knowledge may become its settled abode.